Also by Joyce Keller

Calling All Angels!
57 Ways to Invite an Angel into Your Life

An Astrological Guide to Your Guardian Angels

Your Angel Astrology Love Diet

Your Angel Astrology Guide to Health and Healing

Seven Steps to Heaven:
Contacting Those You've Loved and Lost
in Seven Easy Steps
(forthcoming)

THE
COMPLETE BOOK OF
Numerology

Joyce Keller and Jack Keller

ST. MARTIN'S GRIFFIN
NEW YORK

www.stmartins.com

Design by Ellen Cipriano

ISBN 0-312-25266-8

First Edition: June 2001

10 9 8 7 6 5 4 3 2 1

With gratitude to God,
His angels, and our loved ones

CONTENTS

ACKNOWLEDGMENTS

A big thank you to our family and friends for kind, loving encouragement, particularly Elaine, Jim, Dr. Scott, Grace, John, Joe, Lee, Don, Eileen, Dr. Diane, Frank, Lorraine, Steve, Johnny, Jane, Leonard and Fred.

Unfailing gratitude to our agent, June Rifkin Clark, our editor, Keith Kahla, and Teresa Theophano. Bouquets to those celebs and producers who opened media doors—Oprah Winfrey, Regis Philbin, Soupy Sales, Joan Rivers, Joan Hamburg, Joey Reynolds, Sally Jessy Raphael, Ricki Lake, Geraldo Rivera, Richard Bey, Mary Duffy, Marvin Himelfarb, Ray Curry, Jose Pretlow, Kris Soumas, Connie Kamanis, Joey Alcarese, Linnea Leaver, David Bernstein, Richard Levenson and Dr. Norman Orenttreich.

FOREWORD

The universe, the world and our lives are interwoven with numbers and with numerical values. Sports scores, the stock market indexes, and sales prices are just a few of the numbers with which we are involved every day. Our children's test scores and the distance to grandma's house in miles or travel time (and the gas mileage we will get) are some others. Our modern technical/industrial/commercial way of life depends on numbers, values and calculations from the simplest addition to the most advanced mathematical processes imaginable.

Aside from the numerical values of the ten integers we use to represent all quantities, there is an inherent characteristic or vibration to each of them that operates at a more subtle and mystical level than our everyday, mundane usage. From ancient civilizations until the present many people have utilized numbers for greater understanding and accomplishment.

Is there any validity to any of this? Is it all just a lot of nonsense? Was it thought up and used by frustrated math students who couldn't get past basic algebra? Is it simplistic pap? Or is it just possible that there is some genuine validity to it? If so, do you have to be psychic or intuitive to be able to use it correctly? Do you have to spend years learning how to master numerology? Will people think you're weird and strange, or just eccentric and superstitious?

This book, *The Complete Book of Numerology*, answers these questions, and more. It clears up a lot of the misconceptions surrounding this art. It demonstrates the easiest, most straightforward techniques for understanding and using numerology.

I feel that I am well qualified to write this book, having given numerology a true test of its merit. Numerology has proven to be a reliable and accurate way for me to help people to understand their own life situations and destinies. I have used it to great advantage while doing on-air readings on many TV and radio shows, such as *The Soupy Sales Show* on NBC, or with Regis Philbin, or while on my own radio or TV shows.

—JOYCE KELLER

INTRODUCTION

Numbers are fascinating. In this book, we hope to share with you the concept that numbers are behind some of life's most intriguing mysteries. Not only are numbers intriguing, but they can also be fun—though this usually only happens after you reconcile yourself to the fact that even though numbers may be a challenge, they can also be your friends.

I also discovered that numbers can be very sexy! I know what I'm talking about. In one of my first jobs, as an engineering assistant, I had crushes on almost all of the hundred and fifty engineers with whom I worked. What a group of lovable nerds! These mathematical geniuses could barely dress themselves. They wore jackets that didn't match their stained clip-on ties; polyester slacks that were too short; white socks with shoes that were muddy and had run-down heels. During a pressing project, many of them forgot to shave, shower, or cut their hair. Their white shirts almost always needed pressing, and they never left home without their pocket protectors, and eye glasses with tape. I swear that I am telling the truth! The bizarre thing about this scenario is that I was able to see past their physical appearances, and go directly to the marvel of their technical minds.

These engineers knew everything . . . not only about numbers but, of course, about the universe! I could ask them anything . . . they would stop whatever they were doing, and stare into space until they had an answer for me. I didn't always understand the response, which usually involved some kind of calculation, but I did love hearing it!

Of course I eventually married the most lovable, most handsome and modest, cleanest, neatest engineer of them all (even though he did wear a clip-on tie), Jack Keller. Throughout our marriage, Jack has been gracious enough to help me through many challenges, many of which were math-related. Of course he also jumped at the opportunity to coauthor this book. Needless to say, the most technical parts were written by him.

We hope that this book will help you to share and appreciate our love for numbers. If there is anything that is too complicated or hard to understand, I didn't write it. Jack did.

The Complete Book of Numerology

Chapter 1.

Basic Overview of Numerology

Your SOUL NUMBER reveals your inner, most private, personal self. It is the underlying motivation that influences your decisions and actions, as well as your subconscious desires and your most deeply inherent attitudes.

Your PERSONALITY NUMBER shows how you express yourself outwardly, your appearance and the image you present, how others see you, your power of attraction and the surroundings you enjoy most.

Your DESTINY NUMBER represents your overall aims and the path you will follow in order to accomplish your life's purpose.

Your CAREER NUMBER shows your talents and gifts, and the types of careers or vocations for which you are best suited.

Your MISSING NUMBER shows your areas of weakness and what is underdeveloped in your nature.

The FIRST INITIAL in your name indicates the most significant quality of your personality and the traits which make you unique in the eyes of other people.

The FIRST VOWEL of your name reveals your instinctive reaction to people and situations.

NUMBERS EXPRESS THE
HARMONY OF THE UNIVERSE

The entire planet hums with what's known as the Schumann Resonance. It is calculated to have a mean value of 7.83 Hz. According to ancient mystics, seers and astronomers, this resonance was referred to as the "grand music of the spheres."

When astronauts ride the space shuttle out of the Earth's gravitational pull, a simulated vibration is given off within the spacecraft to replicate this resonance. This is done to ensure the health and well-being of the craft and its crew.

Do you know that dolphin and whale songs are also measured at 7.83 Hz? This is the vibration of homeostasis, which is human physical wellness or calmness. Perhaps dolphins seem to be smiling and expressing unending joy because they hum along at the rate of universal harmony, 7.83 Hz.

Many people use the "music" of dolphins and whales for healing and regeneration. This is based on the power of numbers—7.83 Hz.

THE POWER OF NUMBERS

Pythagoras, often called "The Father of Mathematics," was correct when he said, "The world is built upon the power of numbers." Born around 580 B.C. on the island of Samos, he believed that the universe is fundamentally mathematical in nature. He taught that if we understand our incredible interaction with numbers, life can work amazingly well for us.

WE LIVE IN A WORLD OF NUMBERS

My introduction to the world of numbers was well before I started school. What was so amazing is that the first numbers I saw and learned to add were upside down! As a young child growing up in Brooklyn, New York, it was often my job to run across the street to Mr. Cohen's grocery store to buy whatever comestibles my family needed. Mr. Cohen never used an adding machine, because he had one in his head! With his glasses far over his nose, he would take a brown paper bag and pencil and add up a column of numbers that would be the total of my purchases. Before leaving home, my mother always admonished me to make sure Mr. Cohen did not make a mistake, and that I come home with the correct amount of change. Of course, this put me in a position that was very similar to that of Ginger Rogers, who had to keep up with Fred Astaire by dancing backwards. I had to add the same column of numbers that we were being charged, at the same time Mr. Cohen added them up with lightning speed, only I had to do it upside down. To my knowledge, he never made a mistake.

My mother was very wise. By the time I started school, I was a mathematical whiz. All I required was that the columns of numbers I was adding were upside down!

NUMBERS CAN OPEN DOORS FOR YOU,
AND GIVE YOU AMAZING ANSWERS!

In 1985, Regis Philbin asked me to come on his show for the purpose of testing my psychic ability. Playing a secret game of "numbers," he had me sit on one side of a wall, and his mystery guest sit on the other. Live, on the air, Regis told me his celebrity's birth date . . . July 6, 1927 . . . 7-6-1927. I repeated the numbers 7-6-1927 to myself . . . knowing it would help me to open the door to knowing the correct answer. It was the only information I was given about his mystery guest. Using these numbers as a focal point, I began to psychically receive certain impressions.

I closed my eyes, and began to give his celeb a little reading. I said I thought it was a female, and added, "I also feel this person is a wonderful mother, with very talented children." After a few other comments about Regis' guest, I began to intuitively get the initials "J" and "L," while realizing she had light hair. I heard a little voice in my head say, "Psycho . . ." Wait, was I being insulted by the world of spirit at such a trying moment? No! I became excited when I realized that I probably knew who his mystery guest was! Starting to perspire profusely, I said a quick, silent prayer to myself, and crossed my fingers behind my back. I said to Regis, "Could it be . . . Janet Leigh?"

The audience screamed and applauded, and Janet Leigh came around to my side of the screen to hug and kiss me. Regis said, "Joyce just brought the house down." I thought to myself, "There's no way I could have done that without numbers!" Knowing the numbers 7-6-1927 intuitively helped me come up with the correct answer.

When *The Merv Griffin Show* heard about what I did on Regis' show, they asked me to do the same thing. It would also be on live

TV, only this time with two secret celebrities! My first inclination was to run the other way, but against my better judgment, I found myself saying, "Yes, I will attempt to do it again!" I could feel myself starting to get new gray hairs.

After much secrecy, and keeping me in a closet before airtime, the moment of truth finally arrived. After Merv introduced me, I walked out onto his set. I was terrified, and could hear my heart beating in my ears. I was in a cold sweat, and felt faint. Merv asked me for some celebrity predictions for the year, which I managed to give him. He then gave me the first set of numbers—the birth date of his first mystery guest, July 17, 1917 . . . 7-17-1917 . . . 7-17-1917 . . . 7-17-1917 . . . I said a silent prayer, and closed my eyes for a moment.

I intuitively felt the person's first name started with the letter "P" or was it "D". . . . No, it's a "P" like in "pickle". . . . No, that can't be . . . why am I seeing a pickle? Oh, God, help me!" Just then, I silently heard in my head, "Not 'pickle,' . . . Phyllis." Hmmmm . . . Phyllis . . . born 1917 . . . I suddenly realized that it might be Phyllis Diller! I thought to myself that she was about the right age. . . . I'm going to say it . . . so what if I make a complete fool out of myself? I have no choice . . . my head is spinning . . . I can't think of anyone else! Help! Someone help me!

"Merv," I said as calmly as possible, "is it Phyllis Diller?" He shouted that I was correct, and he and Phyllis, who was in a disguise, hugged and kissed me, while the audience cheered.

I was not as lucky with my next celebrity guess. Merv gave me the birth date of 7-30-1947. I repeated the numbers to myself, over and over. . . . I silently prayed for an answer. I was tired . . . I wasn't hearing or feeling anything! I wasn't able to guess that Merv's mystery guest was Arnold Schwarzenegger. Merv was a gentleman, and graciously thanked me for being so much fun(!), and for being on the show. I felt terrible, and felt that I had failed miserably. I vowed never to attempt to play this particular numbers game ever again.

LISTEN TO YOUR INTUITION, SO THAT NUMBERS CAN WORK FOR YOU

It has been my privilege to give "predictions for the year" on New Year's Day for Regis Philbin's TV shows. As I was walking out of WABC-TV's greenroom on the way to his set to do his January 1, 1989 show, I received a very strong psychic impression. Even though I was ready to give my predictions for the year, I suddenly found myself receiving one more. . . . "The Berlin Wall will come down this year. . . . The Berlin Wall will come down this year . . . eleven . . . eleven . . . eleven . . . "

"What? What? What are all the elevens? Was the Wall really coming down? . . . Big prediction! But, is it right? Should I say it? When will it happen exactly? Was it right?" What are the elevens? I'm starting to shake now, because I don't know what to do! I suddenly went from having a slight adrenaline rush to having a great big sweat. The next thing I knew, I was sitting next to Regis and Kathie Lee, and having a microphone attached to my dress.

The red lights on the cameras came on, and we were on the air. Regis looked at me, and said, "So, Joyce, what's going to happen this coming year?"

I could feel huge beads of perspiration breaking out on my hairline and running down my forehead.

Thinking to myself, "Please, God . . . let this be correct," I said, "Well, I believe there is a very good chance that the Berlin Wall could come down this year, but I'm not sure exactly when!"

Regis said, "The Berlin Wall. Wow . . . that's quite a prediction!"

To this day, though, I kick myself that I did not trust my intuition enough to add "eleven," or say that it would happen in the eleventh month . . . or that I did not try harder to understand it. In retrospect, I realize that what my guidance was trying to tell me was that the Wall would come down in the eleventh month. The Berlin Wall came down November 9, 1989.

NUMBERS CAN BE FAITHFUL AND RELIABLE, IF YOU UNDERSTAND THEM!

My mother was a great psychic who loved numbers, and she used them to her advantage. She made decisions based on her own particular form of numerology. Many of the major purchases our family made were based on her use of numerology. For example, she knew that we could not live in a house that did not have a "nine" in the address.

When my Dad became seriously ill, and we had to move out of our house quickly, we enlisted the help of my Aunt Josephine. My aunt lived on Long Island, and could help us expedite the process. Aunt Josephine called us and said, "I found the perfect house for you in North Babylon. It's a quick, good deal, and I think you should do it." With Auntie "J" at the helm, we moved overnight from Brooklyn, New York, to North Babylon, Long Island. It was a sale of a builder's model home, in a new tract of land, so the house did not yet have a number.

On moving day, we were told that the address of the house was a number "two." My mother was confused! She was upset. How could we move to an address that was not a "nine?" She refused to unpack our boxes. She was a true numerologist!

The five of us, my mother, father, brother and sister, lived out of boxes for about a month. Finally, a letter came from our town hall. It informed us that our address, for some unknown, unexplained reason, was being changed to a "nine!" My mother said simply, "Now, that's more like it. Now we can settle in. Unpack the boxes!"

"Thank God," I thought to myself, "my mother finally has resolution about this, and we can move in." It may have seemed like a small change to the town, but it was a very big change for us. It's all in the numbers!

THE PRACTICAL USE OF NUMEROLOGY

A number of years ago, my husband and I sold our house because it was too small to accommodate our growing family. In meditation, I asked to be shown where we should move. After three days of asking, I had a dream wherein I saw the numbers, "one-six-eight." 1-6-8 . . . where? What town?

After running errands, I sat in my car, still wondering about where I would find "1-6-8." A little voice in my head softly said, "Look behind Sears. . . ." Behind Sears? Sears? Was I starting to lose it? I didn't think we could afford a house there. Optimistically, I decided to drive on the street directly behind the shopping center, just in case. . . .

After a couple of minutes, I passed a house with a big "For Sale" sign on the front gate. The number was 1-0-6-8 . . . hmmm . . . not 1-6-8, but 1-0-6-8. . . . That's pretty close! I stopped my car, and got out. A woman was sitting on the front step. I told her I was interested in seeing the house, and asked her the price.

She then answered, "The owners just died, and we have to have a quick sale. There are five children involved." She then mentioned a ridiculously low price, and offered to show it to me. I couldn't believe it. The house was perfect. It had four bedrooms, two baths, a great yard, and was perfect for us. The price was so reasonable that, even though I love to bargain, I didn't try to get the price down. We were thrilled to buy the house, and moved in a short time after that. We lived happily in that house for many years.

If we ask sincerely for guidance, our guidance will almost always offer us something pertinent but it may not always be easy to understand and interpret. Just listen carefully, and try to remember what you are told. It can often be very subtle, or in a dream. Keep a note pad and pen by your bed, or a little tape recorder. Listen carefully . . . you will be guided, and often by the numbers!

WHAT IS NUMEROLOGY?

The principle of numerology is that all of the numbers that relate somehow to your life can be reduced and simplified down to one single number, except for the numbers eleven and twenty-two.

Every person has a special number that influences and controls his or her life. If you have studied astrology, you'll find this very similar to the idea of an astrological sign. Instead of being, say a Leo, you may find that you are a "number 6" person.

This number, or in many cases, a series of numbers, may repeat over and over in many different situations of your life. The numbers that repeat frequently in my life are three, five and seven. The first car I bought had only those three numbers in the license plate. These three numbers usually reappear as my "lucky" numbers. They have often shown up in my phone numbers and addresses. Pay attention to the numbers that seem to consistently reappear in your life. It's not an accident. They reflect and manifest your soul's energy or vibration.

Numerology is the study of the numbers inherent in our

names, birth dates, and the other significant objects and events that surround us, and their meanings and effects. Since the beginning of time, human beings have recognized that the names and numbers which are associated with things are very important. Success in a variety of ventures in life relies on knowing how many of something is appropriate, how much is good and how much is not. Additionally, numbers have properties that descend from the structure of our minds, and from the structure of our universe, and the vast majority of religions and cultures attach mystical significance to certain numbers.

Many people find that numerology provides very valid insights into their lives and the things happening to them. Numerology attempts to analyze the numerical information around us, and makes a determination of the implications and associations that these numbers have. Numerology uses techniques common in data transmission and cryptography (the art of writing or deciphering messages in code) to derive, from the numbers of your birth date and the letters of your name, numbers and structures of numbers that reflect or contain the influences of each individual digit of the base information. Our culture holds, and numerology has found, that each number has certain implications, which hold influence over us.

BELIEFS AND SUPERSTITIONS
AROUND NUMBERS

Is there any validity to the bad hype that numbers, such as thirteen, often have? Is Friday the thirteenth really a bad-luck day? Why do most office and apartment buildings avoid having a thirteenth floor? Are thirteen at a table really bad luck? Does someone always die when thirteen people dine together?

Professional numerologists say that there is no validity to thinking or believing that the number thirteen is bad luck . . . especially because it really is only the number four! My feeling is that if you believe something is true, and you believe it strongly enough, sooner or later it will probably prove to have some validity in your life.

I believe that much of the bad hype surrounding the number thirteen has to do with the Last Supper, when Jesus and His twelve disciples were present. I doubt if thirteen was considered an unlucky number before that event. One more thing that I know for certain is that my mother never allowed thirteen people to sit at the table. She felt that having thirteen at the table was a virtual death sentence for someone present, or someone close to those present, or possibly a friend or neighbor. I wasn't about to test her theory. My mother always knew best.

In this book we will be discussing the basics of numerology and another type of numerology, called "Gematria." Gematria taught that if the numerology of a name determines the meaning and mystical significance of the name, and of the thing it describes, then other things with the same numerological attributes should be comparable in their basic principle. For instance, the number of the devil or demons is 666, and if you look you will find that the only Biblical passage numbered 6:66 is John 6:66, which is, "From this time many of His disciples turned back, and no longer followed Him." Is this just a coincidence or an accident? Do you think that 666 holds any real message or significance? Do you think that the Antichrist will have the "Mark of the Beast," or 666, tattooed in his/her hairline, or somewhere on the body? These questions are part of the theory of Gematria.

THE EARLY USE OF NUMBERS

From 8000 B.C. to 3300 B.C. in lower Mesopotamia, hunter-gatherers, or mesolithic people, used clay tablets to assist in counting and transmitting their numerical and bookkeeping information. This early math gave rise to the later form of Sumerian writing. Interestingly enough, accounting clearly predated other forms of writing, making accounting and the use of numbers the oldest documented profession.

In 6000 B.C., the early brewing of beer required very strict attention to measurements, according to early beer-brewing traditions and rituals.

From 3300 to 2050 B.C., the Sumerians of Mesopotamia used pictographs before they used cuneiform markings in their early math. Our modern expression of circular or angular measurement and time is based on the Sumerian legacy of sixty degrees, minutes, and seconds. The word "dozen" derives from the Sumerian word meaning "a fifth of sixty."

In 3100 B.C., near what is now Salisbury, England, there was another important mathematical expression, in the first phase of building Stonehenge. It was a large circular ditch, with fifty-six pits around it. It represented the number that is twice the number of days in a sidereal month . . . so it might be that the pits were related to the days in the month.

From 2700 to 2200 B.C., the Egyptians of the Old Kingdom Era developed a 365-day calendar which, of course, we are using to this day. Pyramids near Cairo, which are believed to have been built between 2600 and 2500 B.C., are an early indication of the understanding of geometrical and mathematical skills.

Around 2100 B.C., near Salisbury, England, the second phase of building Stonehenge occurred. It was important because a thirty-five-ton stone was carefully placed so that it marked the rising of the sun on the summer solstice, June 21.

According to the American astronomer Gerald S. Hawkins, Stonehenge was used to predict the summer and winter solstices, the vernal and autumnal equinoxes, and eclipses of both the sun and moon. In addition, a variety of other information pertaining to the sun and moon could be predicted with remarkable accuracy. Hawkins concluded that Stonehenge functioned as a means of predicting the positions of the sun and moon relative to the Earth, and thereby predicted the seasons and perhaps also acted as a simple daily calendar.

From 2000 to 1700 B.C., the Babylonians of Mesopotamia inherited the cuneiform number system from the Sumerians. It was used to record interest payments, loans and deposits. These people understood the principle of the Pythagorean Theorem, and could even solve algebraic problems.

Around 2000 B.C., the Hittites invaded the Middle East, calling cuneiform their own, after learning it from the Hurrians.

Also around 2000 B.C., the Mayans of Central America used a numerical system that was very advanced, and included a symbol for zero.

Around 1900 B.C., the Egyptians fleshed out their numerical system with an understanding of base ten, which used additive symbols.

The Greek mathematician Euclid, who lived around 300 B.C., contributed the classic work, *Elements,* which is a comprehensive treatise on mathematics. It is thirteen volumes on such subjects as plane geometry, proportion in general, the properties of numbers, incommensurable magnitudes, and solid geometry. Euclid made several original discoveries in the theory of numbers. Even today we use a modified version of Euclid's *Elements.* It forms the basis of high school instruction in plane geometry.

PYTHAGORAS, THE FATHER OF MATH

Pythagoras is credited with being the first pure mathematician, and he revered numbers and numerical relationships, seeing them as being the essence of the material world around us. He was not only a mathematician; he was trained in the Greek way of thought, which taught that people should pursue many interests. He was very interested in all aspects of the world, and he and his followers influenced, and often revolutionized, geometry, algebra, music theory, acoustics, astronomy, literature, religious thought and magical works.

Pythagoras believed that reality was ordered, that there was a fundamental order to the cosmos and that everything was intended to follow an archetype of perfection. There was order to music, astronomy, mathematics and numbers, and throughout all of society. Pythagoras believed that reality was fundamentally mathematical in nature and that numbers controlled and made up the essence of what we experience every day. He founded the Pythagorean Brotherhood, dedicated to the reformation of life to a new standard of morality. They were strongly religious and believed that it was possible for the soul to achieve union with the divine, and that symbols could have mystical significance and powers. He believed that the forms of nature could be described and generated using integers, or whole numbers, and ratios of integers, having values such as $\frac{1}{2}$, $\frac{2}{3}$, $\frac{3}{4}$ . . . They saw a parallelism between the creation of the world from void and nothing, and the beginning of numbers with the zero, with the one appearing in the void, and giving rise to all other numbers. Pythagoras also believed that the dynamics of the universe derived from the interactions of opposites, which perhaps derived from his religious thought.

Aristotle tells us: "For as the Pythagoreans say, the all and all things are defined by threes; for end and middle and beginning constitute the number of the all, and also the number of the triad." Pythagoreans noted that the sum of the first four numbers (1+2+3+4) was ten, which could be symbolized by an equilateral triangle with three units of lengths on a side. They called this triangle the "Tetraktys" which means, approximately, "fourness." It has been also referred to as "the sacred decad." Pythagoras noted its correspondence to the end of the point (1), line (2), triangle (3), and tetrahedron (4), as measuring a position, a magnitude, an area, and a region of space. The Pythagoreans also taught that the number seven was a crisis number and that all days that could be divided by seven were critical.

The Pythagorean Theorem is named after Pythagoras. This theorem holds that for any right triangle, the square of the length of the long side is equal to the sum of the squares of the short sides. Pythagoras and the Pythagoreans were not the first to be aware of the relationship, but they are believed to be the first to prove it. At this point, their name is associated with it, and it is being taught to every schoolchild. Not that Pythagoras was not a brilliant man, and his followers intelligent and great contributors, but one might think that this was his greatest contribution.

Pythagoras also discovered irrational numbers—nonrepeating decimals that could not be expressed as fractions—and this presented a problem for the Pythagoreans, controverting their belief that everything could be expressed as simple ratios of the integers. They must somehow have been able to accept a certain amount of "irrationality" as the Pythagorean Theorem generates irrational numbers in many of its solutions. The Pythagoreans also derived the area of a circle using a concept of a large number of infinitesimally small triangles . . . not so far from modern calculus.

MATH BECOMES MORE MODERN

Plato, a great mathematician, founded an academy at Athens that survived until 529 A.D., when all non-Christian schools were closed by the Emperor Justinian.

In Jesus Christ's life, his prophecies and works included many numerological references and elements.

From 100–170 A.D., Ptolemy counted and documented 1,022 stars, and proposed a universe centered on the Earth, with the stars and heavenly bodies fixed in crystal sheets that moved about the Earth.

In 300 A.D., the *Sefer Yezira* was written, which was the basis for the emergence of Kabbalism, or Cabalism. At that point, a form of Jewish mysticism emerged. It is based on the contemplation of the ten aspects of God, as revealed in the Creation, and in the twenty-two letters of the Hebrew alphabet. The Hebrew language makes use of the Gematria, which is numeric interpretation . . . the basis of modern numerology.

Around 1100 A.D., Adelard of Bath brought some of the lost knowledge of Greek math back to Europe from Islamic countries, where it had been preserved and supplemented by the work of Islamic scholars.

In 1582 A.D., John Dee and Edward Kelly derived a numerological system from their communications with angels that they encountered in visions.

In 1887 A.D., the Hermetic Order of the Golden Dawn, formed by Samuel Mathers, William Westcott, and William Woodman, worked to advance Enochian mathematical concepts.

THE MYSTERY OF THE PYRAMIDS

The remains of about seventy pyramids may still be seen in Egypt and the Sudan and perhaps the most outstanding group of pyramids in Egypt is at Giza, near Cairo. The largest, the Great Pyramid, was built as the tomb of the pharaoh Khufu and is one of the Seven Wonders of the Ancient World. How were the pyramids built? When built, the Great Pyramid measured 481 feet in height, with a square base of 759 feet on each side.

The prototype of the true pyramid in Egypt was the step pyramid, so called because its successive layers of massive stone suggests a series of enormous steps. The most famous and best preserved of the step pyramids is that of Saqqara, near Cairo. It was built around 2700 B.C.

The mathematical equations used to build the pyramids are very advanced and esoteric. Perhaps the most amazing fact about the pyramids is that the ancient Egyptians knew how to combine mathematics and knowledge of mysticism. Through architecture, mathematics, geometry and the ancient science of "measuring," man can know the secrets of the universe as encoded in these ancient structures. The geometry and mathematics encompassed in the amazing pyramids, as well as the belief in prophecies surrounding the inner chambers of the Great Pyramids, are esoterically encoded in mathematics.

A PIECE OF THE PHI

The knowledge of ancient Egyptian civilization united mathematics, art, religion and science. Though copied through the ages, much of the glory of the ancient Egyptian culture is ignored today. For example, the so-called Golden Section number, phi, is a mathematic function approximated as 1.618 and is found in the geometry of the Temple of Luxor and parts of the Great Pyramid. It also appears in later construction such as the Parthenon in Athens and some Gothic cathedrals, but not in modern structures. Modern mathematicians are starting to deduce that phi may have deeper meaning than mere geometry, because its inception was so steeped in mysticism.

Like Stonehenge, the pyramids are cloaked in mystery and are masterworks of mathematics expressed in stone.

THE TEACHINGS OF INITIATES
OF SOUL TEACHINGS AND WISDOM
WERE BASED ON NUMBERS

Esoteric, or secret, teachings of the mysteries of the soul and of life, were taught in ancient times in mystery schools. Initiates, or students of the mysteries, were part of the School of Athens. Much of the teachings that were offered centered on the work of Plato and Aristotle at the Hall of Learning. Pythagoras and Euclid also taught about the mysteries of life. The mysteries were often explained or demonstrated on a clay slate, usually from a mathematical angle or viewpoint.

The purpose of the mystery schools was to help students unite with the higher, or most godlike, part of themselves.

DOES GOD SPEAK TO US IN CODE?

The ancient science of Gematria is based on a hidden code in numbers, as used by ancient Egyptians, Hebrews and early Christians. For example, it has come down through the ages that 888 is the number of Jesus in the Holy Scriptures, 444 is God's number and 666 is the number of what's known as the Beast.

THE SECRET OF NUMBERS AND HARMONICS

According to ancient Greek philosophy, the musical scale discovered by the philosopher Pythagoras was seen as the Utopian mode of the harmonic order behind the structure of the cosmos and human existence. Through proportion and harmony, the musical scale bridges the gap between two extremes. It encapsulates the most fundamental pattern of harmonic symmetry, and demonstrates how the phenomena of nature are inseparably related to one another through the principles of reciprocity and proportion, where each part of the whole receives its just and proper share.

Chapter 2.

The Meanings of the Numbers

The primary numbers in numerology are one through nine. In addition, most numerologists agree that there are two master numbers—eleven and twenty-two—that must be taken into account without being broken down to a single digit. The four odd numbers, one, three, five, and seven are considered spiritual in nature. The four even numbers, two, four, six, and eight are considered material in nature. Number nine is considered a balance or harmony between the spiritual and the material. The master number eleven has the nature of inspiration, or awareness of the spiritual. The master number twenty-two involves application, or bringing the spiritual into the material. Some numerologists include "thirty-three" as a master number. A number of highly respected authorities do not include it. In this book, we will be considering only "eleven" and "twenty-two" as master numbers. Every number has both positive and negative sides, which are pointed out so that destructive pathways may be avoided. For each, a basic positive and negative keyword is given, in addition to a group of keywords that describe the nature of the vibration of the number. A description of the type of person who has this number predominate in his or her birth date or name follows, as well as a list of careers or occupations that would be most suitable. Also included are the numbers that best relate, favorable days, the associated astrological body (Sun, Moon or planet) and the most suitable colors. (For birthdate numbers see chapters 4 and 6; for name numbers see chapter 7.)

Number One—Individuality versus Selfishness

Keywords: Positive—Leadership, independence, originality, dynamic, hard-working, courageous, decisive, intellectual, creative, ambitious and strong-willed. Negative—Stubborn, selfish, impatient, intolerant, reactive, egotistical, headstrong, self-centered, irrational, antisocial, tyrannical and unstable.

Number one relates to starting new projects or new relationships and cutting off the past. A number one person is a pioneering type or strong individualist who gets things done and provides leadership for others. One is ruled by the Sun and is masculine in nature. Number one people are mainly mental types and tend to be loners. If they lead or interact with others without being dominant, egotistical or insensitive, and with the purpose of benefiting others as well as themselves, they will succeed. They can also fail if they become lazy, indecisive or lacking in self-confidence. They must avoid both extremes of iconoclastic or tyrannical behavior and stagnation from overdependence on others. They need the support of a patient, loving spouse in a secure and comforting home.

Career or Occupation: Management, executive, inventor, lawyer, writer, designer, engineer, business owner, medical doctor, teacher, lecturer, composer, artist, musician, military officer, movie director or producer, sales manager, TV or radio station manager, foreman, department head, editor, principal, production manager, program director, buyer, religious leader or any unique area requiring originality or innovation.

> Number one people relate well to those in the
>   vibration of two, four and seven.
> Favorable days: Sunday and Monday
> Polarity: Positive
> Astrological body: Sun
> Element: Fire
> Color: Red

Number Two—Teamwork versus Subservience

Keywords: Positive—Considerate, receptive, patient, sensitive, intuitive, cooperative, diplomatic, friendly, adaptable, imaginative and charming. Negative—Hypersensitive, moody, deceptive, indifferent, obsequious, careless, dishonest, pessimistic and sullen.

Feminine in nature and ruled by the Moon, number two is tactful, gentle, understanding, adaptable and wise. People with number two predominant combine well with the masculine number one person. Harmonious relationships, home, family and beautiful, peaceful surroundings are important to number two people. They excel at diplomacy and the ability to handle others. They are very much the peacemakers. Number two people should work for or with others. They are best in cooperative situations working and interacting with other people. It's important for them to avoid being pushovers who accept anything dished out to them. They can also become too detail-oriented and worrisome.

Career or Occupation: Diplomat, banker, consultant, lawyer, accountant, treasurer, bookkeeper, appraiser, politician, musician, artist, homemaker, business partner, bank or store clerk, food industry, chef, engineer, real-estate agent, hotel industry, work of a religious nature or for a religious organization, and with products or services of feminine nature or dealing with females.

Number two people relate well to those in the
    vibration of one and seven.
Favorable days: Sunday and Monday
Polarity: Negative
Astrological Body: Moon
Element: Water
Color: Orange

Number Three—
Expressive versus Self-involved

Keywords: Positive—Self-expressive, spiritual, creative, artistic, sociable, talented, imaginative, good-natured, creative and joyful. Negative—Egotistical, extravagant, wasteful, shallow, gossiper, jealous, intolerant and hypocritical.

A number three person is usually carefree, optimistic and

happy. These talented people usually excel in writing and speaking. Creative outlets are important and can involve dancing, singing, dramatics or some other artistic endeavor. This number is ruled by Jupiter, the planet of abundance and expansion so a three person must not be limited in his or her expression, friends, social life or career. Success comes to those who express their gifts for the benefit of others as well as for themselves. If your talents are stifled or left to wither on the vine, you can become depressed and pessimistic, bringing gloom to others as well as yourself. Guard against being too restless, worrisome, and failing to stick with projects to completion. Don't let your ego or self-involvement lead you to vanity, boastfulness, jealousy or intolerance.

Career or Occupation: Entertainment industry, music, singing, dancing, creative arts, writer, actor, lecturer, designer, missionary, chaplain, church administrator, lawyer, judge, politician, theater manager, community organizer, social worker, dress designer/maker, real estate, stock market, business person, sales, advertising, chef, library, publishing, printing, aviation, jeweler, food industry, toys, amusements or any area of self-expression.

Number three people relate well to those in the
    vibration of six and nine.
Favorable day: Thursday
Polarity: Neutral
Astrological Body: Jupiter
Element: Fire
Color: Yellow

Number Four—Productive vs. Shiftlessness

Keywords: Positive—Practical, organized, orderly, hard-working, enduring, devoted, punctual, conservative, methodical, cooperative, patient and economical. Negative—Earthbound, materialistic, opinionated, stubborn, narrow-minded, slow, vulgar, shiftless and limited. These strong-willed, serious people, when they have a positive outlook, will stick with the job until complete. They advance their own soul development through hard work and service. A number four person is very much the opposite of the carefree, enjoyment-oriented number three individual. The number four people are builders who are best at attending to details in an established routine and expect to work hard to achieve. They don't like unforeseen change and can appear rather dull due to their narrow-minded outlook. They must guard against being too opinionated, stubborn, stern and meddlesome. A person under strong influence of number four must avoid rebelling against limitations and restrictions, which can lead to a state of resentment, self-hate and shiftlessness. However, if a "four" person accepts his or her state in this lifetime and works patiently with system and order, especially in service to others, he/she will achieve great strides in soul development. We feel these individuals to be very much on a path of karma yoga, the yoga of work and service without concern about personal return, which is one of the most effective means of spiritual development.

Career or Occupation: Construction, contractor, real estate, technician, office worker, shopkeeper, retailer, importer, salesman, engineer, craftsman, chemist, farmer, manager, rancher, military, instructor, campaign manager, agent, mechanic investigator or involved with any products or services of a useful nature.

Number "4" people relate well to those in the vibration
   of 2 and 8.
Favorable days: Saturday, Sunday and Monday
Polarity: Negative
Astrological Body: Earth, Sun
Element: Earth
Color: Green

Number Five—Freedom vs. Restriction

Keywords: Positive—Freedom loving, imaginative, change, variety, travel, adaptable, versatile, intellectual, quick-witted, adventurous, independent, sociable and inquisitive. Negative—Careless, vagrant, irritable, irresponsible, vulgar, lecherous, deceitful, and dissipative.

Number five people are quick in thought and action, progressive thinkers and hate to be tied down to routine. They are ruled by the mental planet of Mercury and must use their bright minds in creative and innovative ways to be truly happy. Number five individuals are best in situations of change, communication and opportunities to capitalize on their own talents. These people are sexually magnetic and are strongly drawn to people of the opposite sex, which can get them into trouble if they succumb to irresponsible, lecherous or overindulgent behavior. They must also guard against sensationalism, procrastination and perverse or untrustworthy behavior. Overindulgence in alcohol or drugs could also be a problem.

Career or Occupation: Advertising, selling, travel, communication, creative arts, promoter, transportation, investment broker, actor, lawyer, entertainer, investigator, reporter, shipping, interpreter, lecturer and teacher.

> Number five people relate well to those in the
> vibration of five, and also people in general.
> Favorable day: Wednesday
> Polarity: Neutral
> Astrological Body: Mercury
> Element: Air
> Color: Tan

Number Six—Responsibility versus Neglect

Keywords: Positive—Service, harmony, companionship, home, romance, conservatism, idealism, music, beauty, dependability, marriage, stable, practical, fair and understanding. Negative—Stubborn, selfish, dogmatic, obstinate, irresponsible, domineering, skeptical and egotistical.

These stable, reliable and conscientious number six people are also artistic and compassionate. They are very good in positions of service and responsibility. This number relates strongly to both marriage and divorce. They have a need for beauty and harmony in their surroundings and have a flair for color and art with considerable artistic ability. Success depends on their diplomatic skill in handling people and being of service to others. They must guard against being narrow-minded and stubborn as well as jealous. Matters of the home and marriage need to be especially well cared for. Beware of developing a domineering, cynical or meddlesome attitude.

Career or Occupation: Interior decorator, artist, designer, landscaper, educator, medical doctor, dwelling construction, social worker, healing arts, health stores, cook, child care, veterinarian, restaurant or hotel management, nursing home, commodities dealer or investor, clothing and cosmetics.

Favorable Day: Friday
Polarity: Neutral
Astrological Body: Venus
Element: Earth
Color: Blue

Number Seven—Knowledge versus Confusion

Keywords: Positive—Mysticism, wisdom, study, meditation, science, invention, art, intuition, creativity, spirituality, analytical, research, quiet, scientific and truth-seeking. Negative—Cynical, critical, withdrawn, inefficient, sarcastic, deceptive, inconsistent, deceitful and repressed.

Number seven people are generally introverted and thinkers who prefer quiet solitude to companionship and socializing. They are very individualistic, sensitive, perceptive and quiet. They can be very artistic and creative. Number seven people excel in work where analytical ability or research is required. They must guard against being too withdrawn from everyday life and reality. This can lead to overindulgence in alcohol, drugs, or sex, and result in illness. Negative traits can include criticism, skepticism, maliciousness, promiscuity, substance abuse, duplicity and deceit.

Career or Occupation: Researcher, mystic, artist, professor, inventor, scientist, editor, theologian, chemist, lawyer, detective, criminologist, musician, mathematician, cartographer, metaphysical teacher or lecturer, technical writer, minister or psychic.

Number seven people relate well to those in the
   vibration of one, two and four.
Favorable days: Sunday and Monday
Polarity: Negative
Astrological Body: Neptune, Moon
Element: Water
Color: Purple

Number Eight—Success versus Restriction

Keywords: Positive—Money, power, success, authority, finances, leadership, magnetism, determination, ambition, accomplishment, dependability and organization. Negative—Greed, controlling, miserly, abusive, unfair, tyrannical, unreliable, wasteful, impatient, intolerant, and anxious.

Number eight people are energetic realists with good organizational skills and ambition to succeed on the earthly, material level. Eight relates to big business and finance and the people involved. These authoritative individuals have great drive for material success, but can fail if they make money their god. They must combine spiritual and humanitarian considerations with their drive for power as well, letting up on themselves and others. Number eight people usually desire the security, love and affection of marriage, but often are not able to express their feelings or are too busy to take the time. They must guard against this if they are to find true happiness in life.

Career or Occupation: Management, finance, commerce, business owner, broker, manufacturer, CEO, real estate, physician, hospital administrator, promoter, media executive, consulting, shipping, transportation, architect, civil engineer, publisher, nurse, correspondent, judge, editor, insurance agent, coach, explorer and metaphysics.

Number eight people relate well to those in the
    vibration of two, four, eleven and twenty-two.
Favorable day: Saturday
Polarity: Neutral
Astrological Body: Saturn
Element: Earth
Colors: Dark shades of brown, gray and black

Number Nine—Humanity versus Selfishness

Keywords: Positive—Altruistic, spiritual, idealistic, sympathetic, understanding, organized, tolerant, imaginative, leader, broad-minded, humane, generous and magnetic. Negative—Narrow-minded, impulsive, emotional, nervous, frightened, selfish, unkind, unethical, morose, vile and dissipative.

Number nine people are similar to number eight and number one people in that they have drive and ambition to succeed. However, they're generally less materialistic and more compassionate, with a broader outlook on life. They have the drive and courage to be leaders, but excel in service to others and are generally kind and charitable. These individuals should guard against becoming overemotional, quick-tempered, narrow-minded or lacking in direction. Number nine indicates the end of a cycle and can signify the end of a relationship. When in a nine-time period, it's best to refrain from starting anything new, but to tie up loose ends and prepare for the future.

Career or Occupation: Travel, communications, foreign service or enterprise, public service, social worker, writer, teacher, artist, inventor, publishing, movies, importer, hospitals, nurse, doctor, musician, designer, cabinet maker, or counselor.

Number nine people relate well to those in the
   vibration of three and six.
Favorable day: Tuesday
Polarity: Neutral
Astrological Body: Mars
Element: Fire
Color: Gold

Number Eleven—Idealism versus Fanaticism

Keywords: Positive—Spiritual, mystical, humanitarian, intuitive, inspirational, understanding, intelligent, artistic and inventive. Negative—Selfish, dishonest, haughty, lacking direction, miserly, thickheaded, domineering and fanatical.

People under the influence of this master number are generally visionary and ahead of their time, not easily understood by others. They are basically seekers of truth and not beholden to the conventional establishment. They go their own way, sometimes to the extreme of being separate from society. Their success is in finding spiritual truths about life and existence that can be of help to humanity as well as to them. They must guard against extremism or fanaticism, which can not only lead them astray, but also render them useless as far as being a good example to their fellow man.

Career or Occupation: Psychoanalyst, pilot, actor, electrician, scientist, inventor, healer, minister, psychic, social worker, lecturer, diplomat, explorer and evangelist.

> Number eleven people relate well to those in the
>   vibration of two, four, eight and twenty-two.
> Favorable days: Sunday and Monday
> Polarity: Negative
> Astrological Body: Uranus
> Element: Fire
> Color: Pink

Number Twenty-Two—
Universal versus Self-Aggrandizing

Keywords: Positive—Universal, master builder, expansion, idealistic, leader, improvement and practical. Negative—Self-involved, boastful, indifference, complaining, speculation, crime, violence, black arts and insanity.

People under the influence of this second master number are idealists on a grand scale. They can visualize the big picture and build the reality of their ideals. They will succeed if they proceed with courage and maintain a universal and humanitarian outlook. They can fail if they become slaves to their egos and give way to self-promotion or schemes for quick profit.

Career or Occupation: Leader, manager, public works, international affairs, architect, engineer, builder, overseas shipping, buyer, director of large institutions, political position, social work, health industry, religious organizations, writer, public benefactor, professor and reformer.

> Number twenty-two people relate well to those in the vibration of two, eight and eleven.
> Favorable day: Monday
> Polarity: Positive
> Astrological Body: Moon
> Element: Water
> Color: White

Chapter 3.

Using Numbers to Win!
How to Determine Your
Lucky Numbers

YOU, TOO, CAN BE A WINNER!

This chapter is probably the most important chapter in this book, since it will tell you how to determine your lucky numbers, and how to get them to work for you!

BASIC LUCKY NUMBERS

Very often, you will be able to determine your luckiest numbers by observing what numbers most frequently show up in joyful situations. What is your birth date? The birth dates of those nearest and dearest to you? The addresses of homes where you were the happiest? Most prosperous? Your phone numbers? The license plate numbers on cars that you owned or rented that were the most enjoyable? The dates of days that brought you the most joy or satisfaction? If you ever gambled or played Bingo, what were your winning numbers? What about the numbers on winning horses or if you ever played cards or games of chance?

The chances are great that certain numbers have appeared, and reappeared in your life. What about your dreams? Sometimes, when it is our destiny to win at Lotto or other lucky times, we will see those numbers clearly in a dream, or possibly audibly "hear" them called out to us . . . even if there is no one there! Pay close attention to dreams, daydreams, hunches and inspiration. Keep a clean white notepad and pen with you during the day and close to your bed when you are sleeping. If you are given numbers in your sleep, you definitely want to be able to jot them down!

My feeling is that no one wins big at Lotto, or anything, unless they are first told about it in a dream or meditation. If you don't have a hunch, inspiration or lead, don't waste your time and money. Ask in prayer for a lead or direction . . . and then listen carefully to the information you are given. Don't ignore or override direction; don't think it's your imagination; don't try to conjure it up consciously, because for the most part it won't work!

ACTUAL LUCKY NUMBERS

Your most basic lucky number is often your actual birth date. It helps a great deal and often empowers you, and that number, if you understand how your birth date can actually manifest in personality traits.

If you are born on the 1st: Your lucky day is Sunday. Your number, number one, is called the "Monad," and signifies unity and great individuality. You are a natural leader, strong-willed, independent; you like to go your own way and dislike being told that you are wrong.

You have great inner direction, and march to your own drummer. You are a freethinking individualist, often thought of as "Bohemian," usually uninhibited, ingenious, occasionally headstrong, self-confident, bold, spunky, self-reliant, hard driving, and usually confident. It may be difficult to appeal to your affections, but you like others to show you affection.

You are intellectually inclined, and usually have more than one iron in the fire. Your reasoning powers are excellent, and you are a good organizer. Beware of your jealous feelings and your tendency to want to dominate. You need to be a creative pioneer.

You are an innovative and brave groundbreaker, always avant-garde, a pacesetter, trendsetter, trailblazer! You are secretly admired by many, feared by the less courageous. Your lion-hearted courage can pay dividends when embarking on new endeavors!

Born on the 2nd: Your lucky day is Monday. Your birth number, two, represents equality and justice. You are a natural diplomat and work best with others rather than alone.

You love music, rhythm, and dance, and have a natural sense of harmony and appreciation of the fine and beautiful things in life. The right environment makes or mars you, and you must be careful not to indulge in depression or maudlin thoughts. Underestimation or lack of appreciation by others can be a big handicap—always assess yourself fairly, without undue influence from others. You succeed in artistic or business pursuits.

Born on the 3rd: Your lucky day is Tuesday. You are very versatile, gifted and must have individual self-expression in order to keep happy. Social life and friends are the breath of life to you, because you are basically a pleasure seeker. You are a social asset and much sought after.

You are gifted with a keen mind and lots of imagination. You should write, lecture, teach, or find a place in newspaper writing or journalism. Your best outlet is in the intellectual, artistic, or creative field.

Born on the 4th: Your lucky day is Wednesday. You are a very firm, work-oriented person, determined and sometimes stubborn. You do not like to change your mind more than necessary, or your methods, but your gifts lie in a practical field. You are a hard worker, always systematic, loyal and conscientious. You tend to tell the truth even when it is difficult or unpalatable. Sometimes this causes you to create enemies. Your emotional nature is well under control. You do not always get the attention you deserve. You always finish what you start, so any work requiring attention to detail, discipline and stamina would suit you, but basically the business work is best.

Born on the 5th: Your lucky day is Thursday. You are versatile, quick in mind and body. You dislike confinement or restriction of any kind . . . routine patterns are anathema to you. You are one of life's enthusiasts and you enjoy every minute of it. Travel is usually an important part of your life, which your restless nature appreciates.

You are one of life's exuberant people. Any work that keeps you on the go will please you, owing to your enthusiasm. You would make an excellent salesperson or promoter. Your magnetic approach to life will always draw love, romance, and sex to you. Any field of endeavor that brings you before the public eye in some capacity where there is movement and action would suit you.

Born on the 6th: Your lucky day is Friday. You are a home lover, and need companionship, love and encouragement to give your best. Under adverse conditions children born under this number can get into considerable difficulties and lose their confidence. You have a pleasant speaking voice, which could possibly be professionally trained, and you are interested in music and the arts.

You would do well in any group or community affairs, for you are an idealist and an improver of conditions in whatever capacity you find yourself. You excel in the areas of health, beauty, music, the stage or metaphysics.

Born on the 7th: Your lucky day is Saturday. You are introspective, quiet, analytical, and private. Your aim is perfection and the best of everything, for you are discriminating and not easy to know, although you warm up considerably once you get to know a person. You are attracted toward anything scientific, the occult, or things that are hidden. You are probably quite psychic, and sensitive, and should follow your intuition.

Partnerships are not always easy for you, as you are an adaptable, independent person who can never truly be domesticated. Unique and unusual pursuits are best for you.

Born on the 8th: Your lucky day is Monday. You belong in the business world. You have built-in good judgment, poise and the capacity to wield authority. You are powerful, and good at finances. You are your own best accountant and financial adviser. You may have to struggle against difficult circumstances for at least one period in your life.

You love power, money and the impressively big picture. You are not interested in anything small or mediocre. You can even be ostentatious at times. You need some organization to be completely, over-the-top successful. It is within a strong power structure that your own best powers and capacities will reach their greatest potential.

Born on the 9th: Your lucky day is Tuesday. You have both intellect and creative talents, so some broad field of activity is best for you. The number nine is a universal vibration, so it is likely to bring considerable travel into your life. In addition, communication will also be significant.

You have a tendency to be quite impressionable, generous and protective, so you have to beware giving too much attention or credibility to the wrong people. The wider your viewpoint the happier you will be. You can attain great recognition in any artistic or professional field.

Born on the 10th: Your lucky day is Wednesday. You were born to lead! You are independent, and rarely ask for support from others. You know that others appreciate being able to lean on you. Do not try to work in tandem with other people . . . you are supposed to stand apart. The only people you work well with are the people who can work well on their own. You handle several jobs or obligations well, when you are faced with them all at the same time. You are a perfect company or corporate head, as well as the head of any venture.

Your artistic talents are great, and should be cultivated. Individual enterprise is worthy of your pursuit. You have extraordinary determination, and are able to excel in whatever field you choose.

Born on the 11th: Your lucky day is Thursday. Congratulations! This is a "master" number, and a special birthday. You have high ideals and aspirations. Your problem is that you allow your reason to overshadow your psychic ability and intuition. This will not do, because you are very sensitive and psychic, and should listen carefully to your inspiration and hunches.

Because this is a master number, you come under a high frequency or vibration, and have to work harder than most people to keep your balance, especially when you are stressed and strung out. Emotional control and following a moderate path are necessary for your greatest health and happiness. You have above-average intelligence. Meditate; allow your intuition to express itself, so that you may reach your highest potential.

Born on the 12th: Your lucky day is Friday. You have a warm, lovable personality. You are friendly, with a practical mind and artistic or literary talent. Provided your surroundings are sufficiently interesting, and your love life satisfying, you can be a scintillating entertainer and terrific when it comes to promotion or salesmanship.

However, if your love life and friendships are causing you difficulties, and you are discouraged, then you may not reach your greatest potential. You excel in the entertainment or literary world . . . and can become a household name!

Born on the 13th: Your lucky day is Saturday. If you are not careful, you can misrepresent yourself to the world. If you are discouraged or depressed, the world can see you as callous and dictatorial. Occasionally, you find it difficult to express your deepest, most heart-felt feelings. A hard worker, you are ambitious and enjoy organizing and managing others. You have a flair for intricate detail, as well as scientific and mechanical problems. Try to express your feelings with deep emotion. Express what is in your imagination. Cultivate relaxing pastimes such as sculpting and working in clay, as well as listening to music.

Born on the 14th: Your lucky day is Sunday. You are amazingly versatile and dual-brained, which means, of course, that you can use both sides of your brain equally—the left, logical, mind, and the right, intuitive or imaginative, mind. This is basically a quality of genius! You are a powerful builder who can also destroy everything in your path when the occasion calls for it. More than any other birth date, you stand with one foot on the Earth, and the other in celestial zones. You forge an amazingly inspirational link between the two!

You love all that is new, original and untried. Try to avoid overexperimentation in untried areas. You truly understand and express the success of "the sky's the limit!"

Born on the 15th: Your lucky day is Monday. You are genuinely caring, cooperative, giving and sympathetic, always willing to help and carry more than your share of the responsibility. You should try to avoid situations where you are stifled or where you feel suppressed or dominated, because it might affect your health and state of mind. You have great aesthetic sensitivity, and an appreciation of all that is beautiful in life. You desire and need a calm, peaceful, happy home, and a thoughtful, gentle partner who can allow you the freedom to be who and what you are. You function best in an artistic or professional area, particularly one related to the healing arts.

Born on the 16th: Your lucky day is Tuesday. This is a mystical number that vibrates to a high philosophical purpose and spiritual truth. You don't do well with mundane or ordinary situations, and feel impatient and stressed. You are great at inspiring others to reach their most promising potential, and people often turn to you for advice or counsel. Your own latent talents are well worth developing, and lead to your greatest success, most likely in the literary, artistic or musical fields.

Because you are a perfectionist, you may well become irritable and depressed if you fall short of your highest self-imposed standards. You need a relationship that allows you to be independent.

Born on the 17th: Your lucky day is Wednesday. You may experience wide mood and attitude swings when you feel frustrated and unfulfilled. Many of you who are born on this day find yourselves in the medical field. You are sensitive, caring, and deeply emotional. You have a slight tendency to be extravagant.

You also excel in the areas of finance and real estate. Make your own business decisions, since you are capable of representing yourself almost flawlessly. This should serve you very well financially, since you don't take kindly to any form of deprivation.

Born on the 18th: Your lucky day is Thursday. You are an amazingly independent thinker, efficient, and succeed at all forms of leadership. You love intellectual challenges such as crossword puzzles, and succeed at all mind games and debates. You love expressing your humanitarian nature and great love for people and animals. You have an extraordinary respect for all living things, including plants and trees.

You can be critical and demanding of yourself and others, because of your high standards of excellence. You are analytical, and would succeed as a critic or writer. Expect an active life and much travel.

Born on the 19th: Your lucky day is Friday. You have a tendency to do things to an extreme, and often have wide mood swings. You live your life on the edge of a precipice, an emotional one, but you do have the resources that can help you weather all challenges and difficulties.

Expressing your original thoughts, ideas and versatility will bring you success and prominence. Stay flexible, use your incredible ingenuity, and the world will be your oyster! If ever the adage, "Marry in haste, repent at leisure," applied to anyone, it is often people born on the 19th. Avoid rigid patterns and attitudes, so others don't think you fanatical, even though you bring in the highest truths and understanding.

Born on the 20th: Your lucky day is Saturday. You may often feel strung out emotionally, and may find that you cry easily. Your friends, companions and associates are important to you, not only socially, but frequently as business contacts, also. You appreciate security, love home and family, and would do well in family-oriented pursuits. Your capacity for detail will always serve you well, especially with your Argus-eyed sensitivity and awareness.

You have great leadership qualities that can propel you to fame and fortune. Your artistic and musical talents may also be successfully developed. Avoid occasional mood swings that can give you the reputation for changeability. You can achieve great success by using your analytical and scientific talents, along with your knowledge of computer technology.

Born on the 21st: Your lucky day is Sunday. Your greatest satisfaction comes through expression in literature or the arts. You are almost always tactful and charming, but you are a definite individualist who is fiercely independent. Try to avoid a tendency to scatter your forces and waste your energies in too many directions at once. You have a fine sense of aesthetics, and need beautiful surroundings and people around you. Your excellent use of color, line and form help you to create a beautiful home. Love is very important to you, even though you have many emotional highs and lows. You love the literary and educational worlds, and have succeeded very well there. You are a great entertainer and can be quite the social butterfly!

Born on the 22nd: Your lucky day is Monday. This is a tremendous "master birth date." It is powerful, and carries a tremendous amount of responsibility to others. You will leave the world a better place, thanks to your contributions related to improving the public's well-being, welfare causes, and humanitarian needs. Your ideals cause you to look to wider fields of expression than most people. The primary purpose of your birth is the betterment of mankind. You are an incredibly dedicated Good Samaritan. At the highest level of human evolution, you might find yourself functioning at the love and service vibration.

If you feel that you are not up to this kind of responsibility, read the analysis for the number four.

Born on the 23rd: Your lucky day is Tuesday. Your self-sufficiency has always caused you to be admired by those who know you. You are a quick, agile thinker who thinks and acts quickly on his/her feet. Your insight is remarkable, and you have the capacity to diagnose physical problems in the human body.

You usually have a better relationship with members of the opposite sex than with your own, and with older rather than younger people. You have the gift of flexibility of nature, and adapt well to changes in your circumstances and environment.

Because you are so versatile, you can have great success when venturing into the entertainment field or the medical profession.

Born on the 24th: Your lucky day is Wednesday. Your energy can be quite amazing . . . you must always be on the move and active. You never shirk your responsibilities, especially when they are related to family or community. You are genuinely altruistic, and will never refuse anyone who is in need.

You usually have a great deal of imagination and energy, which is often coupled with boundless dedication to whatever you believe in. It is difficult to ruffle you, it takes a great deal for you to lash out and express your anger or hostility. You forgive and try to forget when you are emotionally hurt, but you carry emotional battle scars for years. You know how to handle jealousy, but do have a tendency to do an unreasonable amount of worrying. A good motto for you is, "Let go, and let God!" Many of you who are born on the 24th find yourselves in the educational field.

Born on the 25th: Your lucky day is Thursday. You are amazingly intuitive, when you listen to your hunches. You can easily inspire others. You often conceal your real thoughts and feelings, and are frequently misunderstood. Your need to succeed is vital . . . your self-esteem is dependent upon it. Your shifting moods are contingent upon your ability to achieve your high goals. Try to avoid underestimating yourself.

Your talents are often expressed through your creativity, show business, and salesmanship. Many of you have writing talent. Do not allow your moods to be affected by your achievements or perceived successes. You prefer a quiet residence to the bright lights of town. As a matter of fact, your peace of mind is strongly effected by your area of residence.

Born on the 26th: Your lucky day is Friday. Your primary loves are home and children. Everything else fades by comparison. Many of you succeed as business tycoons because you are excellent organizers and executives. You have great enthusiasm for starting things but do not find it so easy to complete the tasks. It would probably make life a bit easier if you were to delegate responsibilities, or have more continuity and persistence. Your sense of pride, dignity and position is very important to you.

Stay in the present; don't dwell in the past. Meditate; know that you have a vital destiny on the Earth. Don't give in to sadness caused by empathy for those who are suffering.

Born on the 27th: Your lucky day is Saturday. You have extraordinary strength of character, determination, will and high ideals. All of this contributes to the fact that you are a natural for great leadership. Always strive for the top position available, and work to be on your own, never for the position of the underling or of someone who is not in power and control of his occupation.

You can be a very loving and supportive partner, as long as you make most of the decisions. You are very psychic, and you excel in the areas of metaphysics and philosophy. Many of you are also involved in the workings of the human mind. Try to avoid the negative moods that can occur when you are discouraged, namely withdrawal and introversion.

Born on the 28th: Your lucky day is Sunday. You have strong charisma and integrity, with great spiritual leanings and understanding. Those who do not understand your unique personality can consider you bizarre, or out of step. The truth is that this uniqueness is often the mark of genius. You can be dominant and often very ambitious. Many of you born on this day work best in an individual capacity that is within a group, organization, company or network.

What some may consider dreaming, you frequently bring into reality, with an attitude of, "That should show them!" You lose interest upon achieving goals. You love freedom, and often feel frustrated. All things out of the ordinary are of interest to you.

Born on the 29th: Your lucky day is Monday. You manifest a great gift of imagination, and this is often the key to your self-expression and success. Your happiness in strongly linked to your ability to express that imagination and ambition. You excel at metaphysics, psychology, drama, literature, and have a great interest in science fiction. You recoil when put in a position of having to function in a routine or boring position.

You don't cave easily when it comes to expressing your opinions or attitudes, and would be a great debater, or courtroom attorney. You also have a great sense of justice, and will fight to the death for your belief system, or if you feel that a person or animal has been treated unfairly. You are versatile, easily bored and artistically inclined. At times you allow yourself to be spread too thin.

Born on the 30th: Your lucky day is Tuesday. You have strong ideals, and a basic love of social work, social reform and a caring for the "underdog." You will work tirelessly for a cause or purpose that you believe in, and have the ability to create great fervor (or fever!) for an important purpose. You never shirk your responsibilities, although you do have a tendency to spread yourself too thin.

You have the capacity for being a great speaker or orator, and people love to hear you communicate your ideas or belief system. You would succeed greatly in the media, in television, radio or the Internet. Many of you are late bloomers, with your greatest success coming in the latter part of your life.

Born on the 31st: Your lucky day is Wednesday. You are a builder of ideas, concepts or projects. You are a constructive type of person who can work hard to make yourself or your loved ones secure. You are extremely loyal and dedicated to whatever purpose or persons you believe in. You can be stubborn and very disciplined until you see a project or idea through to its fruition. You love travel, particularly when business is combined with pleasure, and you see the prospect of increasing your income or prestige. Your goals are frequently set so high that your MO can be considered unreasonable . . . unreasonable, that is, until the job is actually finished and done in a first-class manner.

You suffer many disappointments because people fall short of your expectations and you are let down. You may find yourself drawn into the health, healing and fitness field. You work hard to create a good foundation for all that you attempt. Success comes to you through your ability to balance the energies and needs of the body, mind and spirit.

YOUR LUCKY NUMBERS
(WITH NO GUARANTEE, OF COURSE, BUT WITH ALL GOOD WISHES!)

If you were born on the 1st, your lucky numbers are
    2, 6, 8, 9, 11 and 16.
If you were born on the 2nd, your lucky numbers are
    2, 17, 18, 28, 48 and 49.
If you were born on the 3rd, your lucky numbers are
    1, 3, 24, 32, 38 and 50.

If you were born on the 4th, your lucky numbers are
6, 16, 22, 26, 45 and 51.

If you were born on the 5th, your lucky numbers are
1, 19, 20, 47, 48 and 52.

If you were born on the 6th, your lucky numbers are
6, 10, 12, 15, 27 and 48.

If you were born on the 7th, your lucky numbers are
5, 15, 27, 35, 44 and 46.

If you were born on the 8th, your lucky numbers are
1, 2, 37, 47, 53 and 56.

If you were born on the 9th, your lucky numbers are
11, 15, 19, 23, 26 and 37.

If you were born on the 10th, your lucky numbers are
5, 6, 17, 27, 34 and 36.

If you were born on the 11th, your lucky numbers are
1, 4, 13, 21, 31 and 54.

If you were born on the 12th, your lucky numbers are
7, 25, 33, 35, 36 and 43.

If you were born on the 13th, your lucky numbers are
6, 12, 14, 17, 33 and 34.

If you were born on the 14th, your lucky numbers are
3, 18, 22, 46, 48 and 49.

If you were born on the 15th, your lucky numbers are
3, 12, 17, 23, 24 and 50.

If you were born on the 16th, your lucky numbers are
5, 26, 32, 35, 36 and 56.

If you were born on the 17th, your lucky numbers are
25, 27, 31, 39, 42 and 52.

If you were born on the 18th, your lucky numbers are
8, 11, 14, 29, 45 and 56.

If you were born on the 19th, your lucky numbers are
2, 4, 17, 21, 34 and 44.

If you were born on the 20th, your lucky numbers are
2, 9, 11, 17, 24 and 30.

If you were born on the 21st, your lucky numbers are
3, 7, 22, 46, 51 and 52.

If you were born on the 22nd, your lucky numbers are
6, 10, 13, 15, 50 and 51.

If you were born on the 23rd, your lucky numbers are
12, 32, 33, 40, 41, and 45.

If you were born on the 24th, your lucky numbers are
4, 18, 30, 31, 39 and 54.

If you were born on the 25th, your lucky numbers are
5, 28, 30, 31, 39 and 55.

If you were born on the 26th, your lucky numbers are
7, 28, 37, 40, 41 and 53.

If you were born on the 27th, your lucky numbers are
5, 6, 8, 25, 38 and 54.

If you were born on the 28th, your lucky numbers are
11, 18, 19, 20, 29 and 53.

If you were born on the 29th, your lucky numbers are
8, 9, 13, 19, 41 and 44.

If you were born on the 30th, your lucky numbers are
7, 20, 42, 43, 47 and 55.

If you were born on the 31st, your lucky numbers are
9, 19, 21, 43, 52 and 54.

HOW TO GET NUMBERS TO WORK FOR YOU!
WINNING AT GAMES OF CHANCE

"Play not for gain, but for sport; who plays for more than he can loses with pleasure stakes in his heart."

—*Herbert*

MY SECRET, POWERFUL,
MONEY-ATTRACTING AFFIRMATION

This powerful rhyme has proven to reliably empower and charge anyone who repeats it silently, and with confidence, before and during gambling experiences:

Regarding winning,
The outlook is sunny!
I just can't stop
Winning money!

Remember, believing is half the battle!

As a prelude to winning at games of chance, I strongly suggest you begin with the simple act of asking in prayer for what you want and need. Know that your prayers are heard, and can empower your thoughts, wishes, needs and desires. I know that asking for money is seriously frowned on by most religions. My question, though, is why should it be? Why is it all right for most religions to tell us that we should not ask for money in prayer, yet we are continuously asked to make generous contributions to their organizations?

My feeling is that there is nothing wrong with asking for what you need, as long as it doesn't come from a place of greed. Ideally, the money should be used for a good purpose. Most important of all, though, is what I call "priming the pump." Priming the pump involves getting financial success and monetary remuneration flowing in your direction.

The best way to get things started is by becoming charitable. Consider making a donation to a religious organization or charitable cause, and do it generously and not just once! Try to give as generously and freely as you can, to the place(s) where you feel it will do the most good. In the Bible, tithing is stressed as an important part of our soul's growth. An ancillary benefit might very well be that our own coffers are filled to overflowing!

✓ LET'S START WINNING!

Begin with a little prayer or another affirmation that will help to financially empower you:

> *Angels of Abundance*
> *Bring milk and honey*
> *My coffer needs*
> *To be filled with money!*

Ask in simple faith for the floodgates of universal abundance to be opened to you, and for all that you need and desire to come pouring into your life. Try to actually "see" money pouring into your life as clearly as possible . . . in through every window, every door. Visualize tons of hundred-dollar bills flowing in through every window, and through every door.

Write out your request for increased prosperity through gambling, and write it as specifically as possible. Your act of writing helps to solidify and manifest your desires. If you need to win a hundred thousand dollars, state this. Don't be shy! Go for it. You may be pleasantly surprised. Be optimistic, positive and don't set ceilings or limitations on what the universe may be able to bring you.

Before you gamble, it can be very helpful to burn a green candle. Place it in a bowl of water, for safety reasons. Pray near it. Ask in simple, humble prayer for what you need.

Before going to sleep, ask in prayer for lucky numbers, and for guidance in your gambling adventures. Keep a notebook and pad by your bed. After doing this with simple faith for a few nights, you will probably be rewarded with some sort of helpful information. Don't trust your memory . . . even if you are sure you will remember. Write any and all numbers down, even if they come to you in a bizarre fashion. For example, I have dreamed about numbers on the leaves of plants, on the sides of planes, and on mountaintops. I have received numbers that looked like hieroglyphics or cuneiform. Use meditation and logic to try to understand the universal language of symbology. Write them down as best you possibly can, and keep your fingers crossed!

PAY ATTENTION TO HUNCHES; USE YOUR INTUITION!

Pay attention to your hunches, and listen to your intuition. But most important of all, don't let your imagination run wild. Try to get to know the difference between genuine intuition, and imagination and wishful thinking! Don't lie to yourself. For example, don't say that you keep seeing the same numbers over and over again on license plates, and that you should, therefore, play those numbers. That may be true, or it may be an overly optimistic, emotional, and probably irrational feeling. Try to tune in to your most profound gut feelings or impressions. Try to know yourself well enough to know the difference between superstition, wishful thinking, and an actual intuitive direction. Listen to your dreams. Write them down. Tune in to the impressions that you receive in moments of relaxation or reverie. If you feel unlucky on a certain day, don't force it, don't press your luck. If you walk into a casino, and it doesn't feel right, walk out. Try another time or place.

IT CAN'T HURT TO CARRY SOMETHING FOR GOOD LUCK!

Carry a religious metal, lucky charm, stone, crystal, amulet, or something that you believe in. Many people have their item(s) blessed. For cleansing of the item, and to purify and raise its vibration, spritz it with holy water, or Florida water (which can be purchased at most religious shops), and keep it in the sunshine for a few days.

DO THOSE LITTLE THINGS THAT MAKE YOU FEEL LUCKY!

People don't hang upside down and stick their faces in the side of a cave to kiss the Blarney stone for nothing! Thoughts are powerful. If you believe in it, it will be more powerful. Trust your hunches. Wear your lucky shirt or tie. We all have one, and you know it works! In addition, take the advice of Sophia Loren, and tie a little red ribbon somewhere on your body. Be positive. Forget about any past negative or nonproductive experiences that you may have had. Mentally surround yourself with only the highest, most powerful, most helpful energy. Expect the magic to happen!

LET THE LAW OF FLOW WORK FOR YOU!

Don't forget to put the "law of flow" into action. Prime your financial pump with acts of charity and financial consideration and generosity. Forget old, petty, or even big, financial injustices that were done to you. Forget the fact that an old friend of yours still owes you fifty dollars, or that your cousin reneged on a financial obligation. Allow the universe to reward you in other ways.

EXPRESS GRATITUDE, EVEN IF YOU'RE UPSET AND THINK YOU WERE UNLUCKY

Always express gratitude before and after any sort of gambling experiences, even if you came out on the short end! You learned something, didn't you? It wasn't necessarily a total loss, if you gambled and lost. You are definitely wiser, especially if you don't forget the experience. Try not to repeat the same mistake(s)! If you win anything at all, express appreciation to God, your higher self, or whatever you believe in. This is important because it is a positive action that sets the correct spiritual vibration for further gambling success.

BET WITH YOUR HEAD . . . NOT OVER IT!

I found the one time I went to a racetrack to be very surprising. Nobody seemed to be having any fun at all. Many people seemed close to having heart attacks or various types of seizures! The cursing, screaming, and fury from the many people holding losing tickets was shocking. Not only were they not enjoying themselves, and not winning, but they were also almost apoplectic. That must have been the crowd that needed Gambler's Anonymous. If you can't afford to lose, don't gamble! If you win, do not, I repeat, do not gamble it away! If you win, keep it. Go get something to eat, and go to a good movie. These are words to live by.

Remember the words of Mark Twain, who said, "There are two times in a man's life when he should not speculate: when he can't afford it, and when he can."

DON'T GAMBLE OUT OF
NEED OR DESPERATION

Being needy sets up a very negative pattern of energy, and makes it almost impossible to win at most games of chance, the track, Lotto, etc. Fear of losing money that you desperately need will block and stop your chances of winning almost one hundred percent. Energy and attitude are everything. Have a carefree, positive attitude, and you will attract more positive, winning energy. Positive forces and powerful energy will help you to "magnetically" draw good fortune to you. Good fortune will always go to a positive person, to a person who knows he or she is a winner!

Know in your heart, mind and spirit that *you* are a winner, and that you deserve to win! Know that this is the right time and place for good fortune to come your way!

Stay positive, but know and keep in mind your financial limits. Set the amount you will gamble, and *under no conditions go one cent over that amount!*

DON'T GAMBLE RECKLESSLY OR HAPHAZARDLY!

You might get lucky, of course, but the chances of you losing are greater when you don't have a plan or pattern. First of all, if you have some sort of a pattern, which you consider, or hope will be, lucky, go with it. When you formulate a pattern or series of numbers, you are sending that arrangement out to the universe. It gives the forces of nature, or spirit, an opportunity for helping you, or working with you. If you send out a series of haphazard numbers, it is much more difficult. Your structuring and creation of a pattern of numbers is a primary way of cooperating with the forces working with you.

KNOW YOUR GOOD AND BAD DAYS FOR GAMBLING

Your lucky days will most likely coincide with your up days . . . those days when you feel especially high, positive, or good. If you feel especially discouraged, despondent, or fretful, pass on gambling. Wait for another day, since negative or down moods are a reliable reflection of what is actually going on in your magnetic field. The chances are great that your down mood will not help your aura to attract good fortune in gambling. Wait for that day when you awaken with a smile on your face and a bounce in your step. It is God's way of telling you that things are all right in your world. Chances are very good that this will be a lucky day for you in many ways.

LET YOUR DREAMS WORK FOR YOU!

To reiterate, I don't believe that anyone ever wins anything of any serious size or amount without a healthy hint about it, most likely in their dreams. Pay close attention to your dreams, keep a record. Just relax and let the information flow into your consciousness . . . effortlessly, possibly not right away, but within a day or so. Relax!

When you sleep, keep a large, fresh glass of water by your bed, as close to your head as possible. Don't drink that particular glass of water. Pour it out when you wake up. During the night it may have absorbed negative energy that should be disposed of upon awakening.

If you can't remember the winning information you were given in a dream, ask for it to be given to you again, in another dream, daydream or meditation.

IT CAN'T HURT TO LEARN TO
READ TEA LEAVES, OR . . .

Our higher minds may very well perceive what your lucky numbers are in the most unlikely of places. Perhaps a tea bag will break as you are drinking tea, or you will find a streak of coffee grounds at the bottom of your coffee cup. When you think no one is looking, relax, and let your eyes go slightly out of focus. (Try

not to do this on a date if the person doesn't know you well. . . .)
Ask yourself what numbers you see in the bottom of the cup. The
chances are that they will be very lucky for you!

My mother was so psychic that she could spot lucky numbers
just about anywhere. If she drained pasta in a colander, and there
were a few strands left in the bottom of the strainer, she would
very excitedly call me. "Joy . . . come quickly . . . do you see what
I see?"

"Yes, Mom," I usually replied. "It looks like a tough cleaning
job!"

"No, no . . . look . . . it's a seven . . . and a three . . . and a
five!"

If I squinted my eyes and really tried, I could usually make out
the numbers. By the time I was about ten years of age, I was seeing numbers, not only in the bottom of pots, but also in dishes
with food, clouds in the sky, a friend's cigarette smoke, and who
knows where or what else. Just about anything might lend a
major clue to winning. It's a very right-brained effort that can pay
serious dividends, once you get the hang of it! Just relax, let your
eyes go a little bit out of focus, and let your brain receive the winning impression.

LUCK-ATTRACTING NUMBERS, DAYS, STONES, COLORS, AND FRAGRANCES, ACCORDING TO YOUR BIRTH SIGN

ARIES—March 21–April 19: Lucky numbers—1, 3, and 5.
Lucky day—Monday. Lucky stone—kunzite or pink spodumene.
Lucky color—red. Luck-attracting fragrance—jasmine.

TAURUS—April 20–May 20: Lucky numbers—2, 4, and 9.

Lucky day—Tuesday. Lucky stone—clear quartz. Lucky color—saffron or orange. Luck-attracting fragrance—geranium.

GEMINI—May 21–June 21: Lucky numbers—3, 7, and 8. Lucky day—Wednesday. Lucky stone—moldavite. Lucky color—canary yellow. Luck-attracting fragrance—peppermint.

CANCER—June 22–July 22: Lucky numbers—5, 8, and 9. Lucky day—Thursday. Lucky stone—amethyst. Lucky color—emerald green. Luck-attracting fragrance—carnation.

LEO—July 23–August 22: Lucky numbers—1, 6, and 8. Lucky day—Friday. Lucky stone—alexandrite. Lucky color—sky blue. Luck-attracting fragrance—orchid.

VIRGO—August 23–September 22: Lucky numbers—2, 5, and 7. Lucky day—Saturday. Lucky stone—fluorite. Lucky color—dark blue. Luck-attracting fragrance—red rose.

LIBRA—September 23–October 23: Lucky numbers—3, 6, and 8. Lucky day—Sunday. Lucky stone—pink quartz crystal. Lucky color—violet. Luck-attracting fragrance—angelica or allspice.

SCORPIO—October 24–November 21: Lucky numbers—2, 4, and 9. Lucky day—Monday. Lucky stone—sugilite crystal. Lucky color—purple. Luck-attracting fragrance—red apple.

SAGITTARIUS—November 22–December 21: Lucky numbers—3, 8, and 9. Lucky day—Tuesday. Lucky stone—carnelian. Lucky color—deep red. Luck-attracting fragrance—gardenia.

CAPRICORN—December 22–January 19: Lucky numbers—2, 6, and 7. Lucky day—Wednesday. Lucky stone—citrine quartz. Lucky color—saffron or orange. Luck-attracting fragrance—almond.

AQUARIUS—January 20–February 18: Lucky numbers—4, 7, and 8. Lucky day—Thursday. Lucky stone—sodalite. Lucky color—golden yellow. Luck-attracting fragrance—vanilla.

PISCES—February 19–March 20: Lucky numbers—2, 5, and 9. Lucky day—Friday. Lucky stone—smoky quartz. Lucky color—deep purple. Luck-attracting fragrance—peach.

GAMBLE AT YOUR LUCKIEST
TIME OF THE DAY

If you accurately know your birth time, or can take a pretty good guess at the approximate time, you stand a very good chance of winning at that time. If you do not know your birth time, the next best time to try to win is noon. After that, midnight works well.

A helpful book that addresses fortunate cycles is the Rosicrucian classic, *Self-Mastery and Fate With Cycles of Life*, as well as Kenneth Dickkerson's *How to Win Games of Chance*.

THE GREATEST SECRET OF WINNING

The greatest secret of winning at anything is to stay positive! Of course I can imagine that you're saying, "Oh, sure . . . I was so positive and sure that I would win when I bought that lottery ticket, and I didn't win! So there!"

Well, of course, you don't always win when you're positive. But I seriously doubt that you can win anything when you're negative! Isn't it smarter, then, to project only positive energy? The universe will respond much more joyfully and abundantly when you are positive.

In Ken Dickkerson's book, *How to Win Games of Chance*, he quotes Gail Howard, who has won over seventy-three lottery prizes in one year, and is the author of *Lotto: How to Wheel a Fortune*. Gail says, "No one should play games of chance because they need to win, since when you are needy you have a great fear of gambling away the money you've worked so hard for."

Ken continues, "That's just the way life works. But it's this very fear that blocks the winning forces."

Gail says, "Thoughts are charged with energy, especially when triggered by emotions. A negative thought attracts a negative response. . . . Therefore, if you have it in your mind, or even joke about it with others, that you are unlucky or a loser, you assuredly will be!"

Remember what Job said in the Bible, "That which I have feared has come upon me." The greatest secret of winning at anything is to expect the best . . . stay one hundred percent positive!

SECRET KELLER TECHNIQUE
TO GET WINNING NUMBERS

This is a tried-and-true, time-tested technique for tuning in to your winning, lucky numbers. The people who have tried it have almost always won with winning numbers.

"The first time I tried it," according to Janine, who works as a news reporter in New York City, "I was amazed. I tried it, and won $100 at Lotto. After that, I tried it a few more times, and always won something!" Then, she cleverly added, "It works so well that I don't feel right about doing it too often. I'm probably relying on 'higher forces,' and don't feel I should test it too often!"

Janine's attitude is within the spiritual parameters of her belief system. It is what she is comfortable with, and therefore, right for her.

For the rest of you, who may believe that the sky is the limit, here is the system. (Remember though, as with everything else in life, there are no guarantees!).

Write the following words in a column on a clean piece of white paper that is on a firm surface, like a notebook or clipboard:

MONEY
CURRENCY
LEGAL TENDER
COINS
STERLING
DOLLARS
GOLD
GILT
CASH
SILVER

Relax, and repeat the following rhyme ten times:

"Money, money
How easily it flows
Into my pockets
As my bank account grows!"

When you are feeling very relaxed, write one number next to each of the ten words. Repeat the rhyme again, if you have to, and circle the quantity of numbers that you need to win.

Put your hands over the sheet of paper. Say "thank you," to the energies involved in helping to create the series of numbers that you received. Good Luck!

Chapter 4

Your Day of Birth

The day of the month that you were born should always be examined when doing a numerological analysis. Each day has its own special quality or vibration. It has long been common in China for labor to be induced in mothers-to-be so that babies will be born on the day that the parents consider auspicious. For instance, a child's birth date may be chosen to honor an ancestor.

Numerologists have long believed that the vibration of the day of birth is not nearly as strong or important as the life path number. (See chapter 6 for life path number.) The day of birth modifies the qualities of the life path. For example, people who have a 7 life path are likely to be quiet and introspective. However, if they were born on the 3rd, 12th, 21st, or 30th of the month they would gain some of the outgoing expressive qualities of the 3, and would be much more communicative than most people with a 7 life path.

THE NUMBERS SURROUNDING YOU

If you were born on the 1st: You are most compatible with people born on the 3rd, 12th, or 20th of any month.

Your greatest challenges come from people born on the 2nd, 8th or 10th.

Your most challenging days of any month are most likely to be the 4th, 9th or 21st.

If you were born on the 2nd: You are most compatible with people born on the 8th, 13th or 22nd.

Your greatest challenges come from people born on the 12th, 23rd or 31st.

Your most challenging days of any month are most likely to be the 1st, 5th or 9th.

If you were born on the 3rd: You are most compatible with people born on the 9th, 15th, or 17th.

Your greatest challenges come from people born on the 1st, 14th or 23rd.

Your most challenging days of any month are most likely to be the 5th, 17th or 30th.

If you were born on the 4th: You are most compatible with people born on the 1st, 6th or 16th.

Your greatest challenges come from people born on the 5th, 9th and 19th.

Your most challenging days of any month are likely to be the 21st, 26th or 28th.

If you were born on the 5th: You are most compatible with people born on the 17th, 19th or 28th.

Your greatest challenges come from people born on the 23rd, 25th or 30th.

Your most challenging days of any month are most likely to be the 14th, 21st or 29th.

If you were born on the 6th: You are most compatible with people born on the 2nd, 14th or 29th.

Your greatest challenges come from people born on the 11th, 23rd or 31st.

Your most challenging days of any month are most likely to be the 3rd, 12th or 30th.

If you were born on the 7th: You are most compatible with people born on the 5th, 18th or 27th.

Your greatest challenges come from people born on the 10th, 13th or 19th.

Your most challenging days of any month are most likely to be the 14th, 21st or 29th.

If you were born on the 8th: You are most compatible with people born on the 10th, 21st or 28th.

Your greatest challenges come from people born on the 9th, 15th or 22nd.

Your most challenging days of any month are most likely to be the 4th, 26th or 29th.

If you were born on the 9th: You are most compatible with people born on the 4th, 19th or 26th.

Your greatest challenges come from people born on the 1st, 2nd or 28th.

Your most challenging days of any month are most likely to be the 3rd, 18th or 23rd.

If you were born on the 10th: You are most compatible with people born on the 14th, 22nd or 30th.

Your greatest challenges come from people born on the 6th, 9th or 12th.

Your most challenging days of any month are most likely to be the 8th, 14th or 25th.

If you were born on the 11th: You are most compatible with people born on the 16th, 23rd or 28th.

Your greatest challenges come from people born on the 11th, 21st or 29th.

Your most challenging days of the month are most likely to be the 1st, 18th or 24th.

If you were born on the 12th: You are most compatible with people born on the 1st, 11th or 24th.

Your greatest challenges come from people born on the 2nd, 17th or 18th.

Your most challenging days of the month are most likely to be the 15th, 26th or 29th.

If you were born on the 13th: You are most compatible with people born on the 8th, 17th or 21st.

Your greatest challenges come from people born on the 10th, 24th or 29th.

Your most challenging days of the month are most likely to be the 11th, 18th or 23rd.

If you were born on the 14th: You are most compatible with people born on the 2nd, 19th or 26th.

Your greatest challenges come from people born on the 12th, 13th or 15th.

Your most challenging days of the month are most likely to be the 2nd, 21st or 29th.

If you were born on the 15th: You are most compatible with people born on the 6th, 13th or 23rd.

Your greatest challenges come from people born on the 20th, 22nd or 26th.

Your most challenging days of the month are most likely to be the 5th, 17th or 23rd.

If you were born on the 16th: You are most compatible with people born on the 10th, 18th or 30th.

Your greatest challenges come from people born on the 2nd, 23rd or 24th.

Your most challenging days of the month are most likely to be the 4th, 25th or 27th.

If you were born on the 17th: You are most compatible with people born on the 5th, 27th or 28th.

Your greatest challenges come from people born on the 3rd, 7th or 17th.

Your most challenging days of the month are most likely to be the 18th, 25th or 31st.

If you were born on the 18th: You are most compatible with people born on the 16th, 22nd or 29th.

Your greatest challenges come from people born on the 13th, 15th or 26th.

Your most challenging days of the month are most likely to be the 8th, 20th or 21st.

If you were born on the 19th: You are most compatible with people born on the 3rd, 7th or 15th.

Your greatest challenges come from people born on the 4th, 25th or 27th.

Your most challenging days of the month are most likely to be the 7th, 18th or 24th.

If you were born on the 20th: You are most compatible with people born on the 14th, 24th or 28th.

Your greatest challenges come from people born on the 5th, 27th or 30th.

Your most challenging days of the month are most likely to be the 14th, 23rd or 25th.

If you were born on the 21st: You are most compatible with people born on the 4th, 9th or 20th.

Your greatest challenges come from people born on the 3rd, 10th or 14th.

Your most challenging days of the month are most likely to be the 16, 18th or 21st.

If you were born on the 22nd: You are most compatible with people born on the 11th, 25th or 30th.

Your greatest challenges come from people born on the 19th, 24th or 28th.

Your most challenging days of the month are most likely to be the 5th, 22nd or 26th.

If you were born on the 23rd: You are most compatible with people born on the 1st, 10th or 24th.

Your greatest challenges come from people born on the 8th, 14th or 26th.

Your most challenging days of the month are most likely to be the 9th, 21st or 29th.

If you were born on the 24th: You are most compatible with people born on the 5th, 12th or 19th.

Your greatest challenges come from people born on the 5th, 15th or 16th.

Your most challenging days of the month are most likely to be the 2nd, 17th or 24th.

If you were born on the 25th: You are most compatible with people born on the 9th, 14th or 18th.

Your greatest challenges come from people born on the 17th, 27th or 30th.

Your most challenging days of the month are most likely to be the 12th, 14th or 22nd.

If you were born on the 26th: You are most compatible with people born on the 15th, 21st or 27th.

Your greatest challenges come from people born on the 4th, 18th or 29th.

Your most challenging days of the month are most likely to be the 7th, 16th or 21st.

If you were born on the 27th: You are most compatible with people born on the 7th, 16th or 23rd.

Your greatest challenges come from people born on the 6th, 24th or 29th.

Your most challenging days of the month are most likely to be the 5th, 17th or 28th.

If you were born on the 28th: You are most compatible with people born on the 3rd, 11th or 29th.

Your greatest challenges come from people born on the 4th, 6th or 28th.

Your most challenging days of the month are most likely to be the 17th, 21st or 24th.

If you were born on the 29th: You are most compatible with people born on the 6th, 17th or 25th.

Your greatest challenges come from people born on the 7th, 16th or 31st.

Your most challenging days of the month are most likely to be the 11th, 14th or 23rd.

If you were born on the 30th: You are most compatible with people born on the 8th, 20th or 26th.

Your greatest challenges come from people born on the 9th, 30th or 31st.

Your most challenging days of the month are most likely to be the 5th, 17th or 29th.

If you were born on the 31st: You are most compatible with people born on the 2nd, 13th or 22nd.

Your greatest challenges come from people born on the 5th, 8th or 17th.

Your most challenging days of the month are most likely to be the 1st, 4th or 30th.

YOUR SOUL MATE NUMBER
FOR THE BEST COMPATIBILITY

The birth date of this person isn't necessarily that of the person who is the most compatible with you, or even the person who is your primary mate. The following birth dates are for people who have the most significant karma or the greatest life lessons to be worked out with you. It is most likely, though, that a relationship with a soul mate is one in which a romantic, loving or sensual relationship is definitely a possibility. It usually involves marriage or commitment. However, a soul mate relationship can also be with someone who is a very good friend, companion, or loving support system. It is very likely that most of us have at least one soul mate per incarnation. As a matter of fact, most of us will have about five or six soul mates per lifetime.

If you were born on the 1st, your soul mate's birth date may very well be the 1st, 6th or 13th.

If you were born on the 2nd, your soul mate's birth date may very well be the 2nd, 10th or 15th.

If you were born on the 3rd, your soul mate's birth date may very well be the 11th, 23rd or 24th.

If you were born on the 4th, your soul mate's birth date may very well be the 14th, 23rd or 25th.

If you were born on the 5th, your soul mate's birth date may very well be the 12th, 21st or 24th.

If you were born on the 6th, your soul mate's birth date may very well be the 3rd, 5th or 22nd.

If you were born on the 7th, your soul mate's birth date may very well be the 7th, 11th or 12th.

If you were born on the 8th, your soul mate's birth date may very well be the 23rd, 24th or 25th.

If you were born on the 9th, your soul mate's birth date may very well be the 3rd, 13th or 21st.

If you were born on the 10th, your soul mate's birth date may very well be the 1st, 2nd or 24th.

If you were born on the 11th, your soul mate's birth date may very well be the 22nd, 24th or 26th.

If you were born on the 12th, your soul mate's birth date may very well be the 14th, 15th or 21st.

If you were born on the 13th, your soul mate's birth date may very well be the 14th, 20th or 28th.

If you were born on the 14th, your soul mate's birth date may very well be the 10th, 28th or 30th.

If you were born on the 15th, your soul mate's birth date may very well be the 8th, 15th or 27th.

If you were born on the 16th, your soul mate's birth date may very well be the 9th, 20th or 25th.

If you were born on the 17th, your soul mate's birth date may very well be the 26th, 27th or 28th.

If you were born on the 18th, your soul mate's birth date may very well be the 5th, 28th or 30th.

If you were born on the 19th, your soul mate's birth date may very well be the 12th, 16th or 19th.

If you were born on the 20th, your soul mate's birth date may very well be the 4th, 20th or 29th.

If you were born on the 21st, your soul mate's birth date may very well be the 18th, 19th or 28th.

If you were born on the 22nd, your soul mate's birth date may very well be the 15th, 17th or 28th.

If you were born on the 23rd, your soul mate's birth date may very well be the 3rd, 5th or 27th.

If you were born on the 24th, your soul mate's birth date may very well be the 3rd, 6th or 8th.

If you were born on the 25th, your soul mate's birth date may very well be the 16th, 20th or 28th.

If you were born on the 26th, your soul mate's birth date may very well be the 4th, 7th or 10th.

If you were born on the 27th, your soul mate's birth date may very well be the 5th, 17th or 18th.

If you were born on the 28th, your soul mate's birth date may very well be the 7th, 14th or 18th.

If you were born on the 29th, your soul mate's birth date may very well be the 8th, 17th or 19th.

If you were born on the 30th, your soul mate's birth date may very well be the 5th, 16th or 19th.

If you were born on the 31st, your soul mate's birth date may very well be the 4th, 6th or 9th.

THE STRENGTHS AND WEAKNESSES
OF YOUR BIRTH NUMBER

If you were born on the 1st, your strengths are that you are goal-oriented, sincere and technically skillful. Your weaknesses are that you have a tendency to be withdrawn, isolated and a bit of a workaholic.

If you were born on the 2nd, your strengths are that you are versatile, adaptable and usually determined. Your weaknesses are that you can be disconnected, unaware and oblivious.

If you were born on the 3rd, your strengths are that you are persistent, concentrated and superior. Your weaknesses are that you can be long-suffering, procrastinating and occasionally negative.

If you were born on the 4th, your strengths are that you are loyal, faithful, generous and proud. Your weaknesses are that you can be too biased, fixed in your opinions and obstinate.

If you were born on the 5th, your strengths are that you are well-informed, hardworking and enlightened. Your weaknesses are that you can be too possessive, dogmatic and detached.

If you were born on the 6th, your strengths are that you are sympathetic, elegant and perceptive. Your weaknesses are that you can be too self-involved, repressed and overconfident.

If you were born on the 7th, your strengths are that you are curious, adventurous and spiritual. Your weaknesses are that you can be stubborn, restless and vindictive.

If you were born on the 8th, your strengths are that you are self-confident, influential and powerful. Your weaknesses are that you can be self-centered, unforgiving and insensitive.

If you were born on the 9th, your strengths are that you are multifaceted, keenly observant and inspirational. Your weaknesses may be that you can be too controlling, inflexible and stressed-out.

If you were born on the 10th, your strengths are that you are creative, confident and positive. Your weaknesses may be that you can be too insulated, possessive and insensitive.

If you were born on the 11th, your strengths are that you are trustworthy, capable and diligent. Your weaknesses may be that you can be too stubborn, rigid and unyielding.

If you were born on the 12th, your strengths are that you are optimistic, uplifting and generous. Your weaknesses may be that you can be too judgmental, impatient and critical.

If you were born on the 13th, your strengths are that you are devoted, hardworking and conscientious. Your weaknesses may be that you can be too impervious to others, unaware and fussy.

If you were born on the 14th, your strengths are that you are daring, courageous and provocative. Your weaknesses may be that you can be too withdrawn, isolated and moody.

If you were born on the 15th, your strengths are that you are dynamic, inspirational and positive. Your weaknesses may be that you can be too extreme, overconfident and manipulative.

If you were born on the 16th, your strengths are that you are patient, success-driven and clever. Your weaknesses may be that you can be too indecisive, defensive and impractical.

If you were born on the 17th, your strengths are that you are persuasive, daring and self-assured. Your weaknesses may be that you are reckless, obstinate and insensitive.

If you were born on the 18th, your strengths are that you are verbally clever, animated and influential. Your weaknesses may be that you are inconsistent, restless and preoccupied.

If you were born on the 19th, your strengths are that you are very controlled, long-suffering and independent. Your weaknesses may be that you are scrappy, possessive and sometimes oblivious.

If you were born on the 20th, your strengths are that you are charismatic, innovative and dynamic. Your weaknesses may be that you are too undisciplined, overly emotional and power-hungry.

If you were born on the 21st, your strengths are that you are deeply perceptive, intuitive and scrupulously honest. Your weaknesses may be that you are too frustrated, addictive and self-abusive.

If you were born on the 22nd, your strengths are that you are generous, caring and perceptive. Your weaknesses may be that you are occasionally negative, critical and unyielding.

If you were born on the 23rd, your strengths are that you are friendly, confident and exciting. Your weaknesses may be that you are often too possessive, authoritative and vulnerable.

If you were born on the 24th, your strengths are that you are protective, generous and magnetic. Your weaknesses may be that you are often too stressed-out, mixed-up and distracted.

If you were born on the 25th, your strengths are that you are versatile, multifaceted and fascinating. Your weaknesses may be that you are often too unsure, judgmental and have a tendency to overreact.

If you were born on the 26th, your strengths are that you are steady, thorough and successful. Your weaknesses may be that you are too emotionally reactive, blunt and impulsive.

If you were born on the 27th, your strengths are that you are virtuous, persistent and imaginative. Your weaknesses may be that you are isolated, undiplomatic and unrealistic.

If you were born on the 28th, your strengths are that you are resourceful, powerful and convincing. Your weaknesses may be that you are judgmental, authoritarian and permissive.

If you were born on the 29th, your strengths are that you are exciting, indefatigable and inspiring. Your weaknesses may be that you are authoritarian, self-righteous and indignant.

If you were born on the 30th, your strengths are that you are unique, creative and observant. Your weaknesses may be that you are intrusive, flighty and complacent.

If you were born on the 31st, your strengths are that you are charming, sure-footed and confident. Your weaknesses may be that you are too passive, complacent and stressed-out.

YOUR CHILD'S BIRTH DATE

If your child was born on the 1st, you should do everything in your power to nurture his/her leadership qualities. This child will try to make a name for him/herself.

If your child was born on the 2nd, you are dealing with a charming, supportive child, who will be a well-thought-of team player.

If your child was born on the 3rd, you are dealing with a sociable, intense child, who would do well in the fields of art and music.

If your child was born on the 4th, you are dealing with a hardworking, humorous, and at times headstrong child, who will not take kindly to too many suggestions.

If your child was born on the 5th, this child will be restless and interested in a variety of activities. Undoubtedly a sociable creature, he/she will be loved by all.

If your child was born on the 6th, you can expect him/her to be very perceptive and expressive, with artistic and creative talents.

If your child was born on the 7th, you will be amazed at the imaginative, perceptive qualities of this child. What may seem imaginary will one day pay dividends.

If your child was born on the 8th, you will enjoy a sociable, virtuous child, with many qualities of generosity and sensitivity.

If your child was born on the 9th, his/her impulsive ways may get him/her into trouble, but with proper channeling will manifest as genius.

If your child was born on the 10th, his/her daring, adventurous ways may one day pay dividends, with altruistic humanitarian expression.

If your child was born on the 11th, enjoy his/her colorful, expressive ways, which might be interpreted as obstinate. This is the key to success in the legal or entertainment fields.

If your child was born on the 12th, his/her generous, outgoing ways will pay dividends, as will his/her wise-as-an-owl personality.

If your child was born on the 13th, you are dealing with a rebellious, yet metaphysically inclined child. His/her breadth of knowledge will always serve him/her very well.

If your child was born on the 14th, his/her challenging personality will serve to put him/her in a position of leadership, and as someone who is an iconoclast.

If your child was born on the 15th, his/her involvement with finances and security should pay dividends, along with his/her inspirational personality.

If your child was born on the 16th, this charismatic child will march to his/her own drummer, even if it seems he/she is listening to you.

If your child was born on the 17th, this daring child will inspire many people in his/her lifetime with his/her courage and tenacity.

If your child was born on the 18th, nurture his/her imagination, and expect to be surprised by advanced expressions of wisdom.

If your child was born on the 19th, this child is not always easy to understand. His/her mysterious ways will eventually amaze all with his/her amazing perception.

If your child was born on the 20th, his/her exuberance will inspire many people in his/her lifetime. A natural leader, his/her charisma will light the way for others.

If your child was born on the 21st, his/her caring, compassionate ways will be coupled with drive and ambition. A winning combination!

If your child was born on the 22nd, you can expect this child to please you with his/her perfectionist tendencies. What may not be understood at first will turn out to be noteworthy.

If your child was born on the 23rd, he/she may at first appear to be a late bloomer. As in the case of the tortoise and the hare, he/she will ultimately make a surprising mark in life.

If your child was born on the 24th, his/her overanalytical, investigative personality may seem unsettling. It is these qualities, when nurtured, which will produce amazing dividends.

If your child was born on the 25th, his/her cooperation and

mental acuity should be a joy as well as a challenge. Encourage him/her not to hide his/her light under a barrel.

If your child was born on the 26th, his/her nurturing, faithful attitude, in combination with his/her fun attitude, can be the key to a life of great success.

If your child was born on the 27th, his/her high IQ, in combination with a clever, socially adept personality, should work well throughout his/her life.

If your child was born on the 28th, his/her disinterest in things of the Earth, and lofty reaching to higher realms, are the keys to power and success in this child's life.

If your child was born on the 29th, his realistic, pragmatic attitude may be an enigma to adults or his/her peers who find him/her to be a difficult but worthwhile challenge.

If your child was born on the 30th, his/her determined, possibly isolated, personality is only half of the picture. The other half is a vibrant, fun-filled, dynamic friend.

If your child was born on the 31st, his/her perceptive ways may not be easily noted immediately. Expect to see a vibrant, electrifying personality, when enthusiastically channeled.

YOUR LOVER OR MATE'S BIRTH DATE

"You split me and tore my heart open,
And filled me with love;
You poured your spirit into mine,
I knew you as I know myself.
My eyes are radiant with your light.
My ears delight in your music.
My nostrils are filled with your fragrance.

My face is covered with your dew,
You have made me see all things shining.
You have granted me perfect ease;
I've become like paradise."
—From the Song of Solomon, in the Torah

Born on the 1st, this lover will never cease to amaze you with an unending array of suggestions. Love and sex with this person will never be boring or humdrum. Get in touch with your own nature before attempting to give in to the challenges of a relationship with a number one type person. There should be an emphasis on physical well-being. Never appear unnecessarily gullible, vulnerable or weak. Try to be ready for new, adventurous experiences.

Born on the 2nd, this lover will be happiest with tranquility and a peaceful evening. The emphasis on a relationship with a number two type person is on pleasure and hedonism. This is the person who will go for moonlight walks with you, and probably enjoy fine dining. Love and sex may not be adventurous, but they will probably be soul satisfying!

Born on the 3rd, this lover thrives on enjoyment, and will tax your imagination as you both try to come up with new, exciting experiences to share. As he/she will probably love animals, you may have to share the boudoir with a variety of furry friends. This relationship can have dreamy, never-to-be forgotten overtones, if the emphasis never strays from pleasure and good times.

Born on the 4th, this lover's idea of a good time is more practical than pleasurable. For instance, you might very well find yourself painting or sanding his/her boat, before you take it out in the harbor. Sex with a number four type person should be sensual, slow and sweaty, with the emphasis on slow. This is a person who savors the pleasures in life.

Born on the 5th, this lover will leave you breathless, and possibly a little bit lonely. The number five type of person is always on the go, and doesn't usually take much time for the simple pleasures of life. There is usually another trip to take, or another commitment. But the time you spend together can be very special, because you won't have time to get tired of each other.

Born on the 6th, this lover will dazzle you with his/her artistic and musical talents. Expect the bedroom to be aesthetically decorated, if not downright lavish. Make sure your taste in food and wine is impeccable, because there probably won't be much latitude for second-rate anything. Expect lovemaking to be sensual and lavish, with an atmosphere of moonlight and roses.

Born on the 7th, this lover will set you back on your heels with his/her knowledge of all things metaphysical, or at least otherworldly and religious. You might find yourself in a relationship with an ascetic, where you find yourself wondering if intimacy will ever become a reality. The way to win over this lover is by reminding him/her that the path to Nirvana is bliss. Proceed to describe to him/her your definition of bliss!

Born on the 8th, this lover becomes orgasmic when he/she smells power and money. The key to this lover's heart is the path of success. When things are not going well, this person is most likely quite incapable of functioning. The way to this person's heart is to tell them that success, money and power are very close, and that going around in a state of tension doesn't accomplish anything. This is a lover who needs deep, relaxing body massages, with warm, sensual oils.

Born on the 9th, this lover likes to find love in strange, unexpected ways and places. Life in the fast lane may beckon to him/her, and you may find yourself actually living out romantic fantasies. Things may move quickly and smoothly with the number nine type of person. You will probably experience and enjoy an impetuous quality to all that is a part of this relationship. This is a person who loves a challenge, and its ensuing rewards.

Born on the 10th, this lover may let his/her frugality inhibit the full enjoyment that could be in the offing. It will be up to you to gently lead and cajole this practical person into loosening up, and flying freely and enjoyably. He/she is selective and discerning, and often very impeccable in his/her tastes. In the bedroom, this lover is patient and cares deeply about pleasing his/her partner.

Born on the 11th, this lover is open and aboveboard about all that brings pleasure to the senses. He/she doesn't beat around the bush, but comes out clearly about what it takes to bring a smile to his/her face. This is usually a hedonistic person without many inhibitions. This person appreciates experimentation, and will be the first to try anything new. This person will definitely keep his/her partner on his/her toes.

Born on the 12th, this lover is a happy-go-lucky type of person. There is very little that doesn't sit well with this person. Experimentation and new ideas are usually welcomed with open arms. The thought that some people like to be married because it keeps them out of trouble definitely applies to this person. Usually, when they make a commitment, it is for the long haul. Their positive attitude usually makes the number twelve type of person an excellent marriage partner.

Born on the 13th, this lover doesn't like settling for second best. When you are out with this person, it might be smart to always look your best. The number thirteen person is usually quite attractive, and expects his/her mate to more than hold their own in the looks department. The number thirteen person also expects the bedroom and living areas to be aesthetic and neat.

Born on the 14th, this lover can slip through your fingers if he/she is bored or loses interest in you. This is the lover who requires fresh, new challenges and ideas to keep things perking merrily. It's truly dangerous to experience any kind of coziness or "settling in" with the number fourteen personality. Keep him/her guessing. Read the novel, *One Thousand and One Nights* for inspiration.

Born on the 15th, this lover likes to get down to brass tacks honestly, and most likely in a hurry. The number fifteen personality is tenacious, and will probably stick around for the long haul. The only thing that might cause this not to be the case is your disinterest or lack of loyalty. This is a person who will almost always accentuate the positive. He/she epitomizes the saying, "There must be a pony in here somewhere . . ." when asked about why they were shoveling through a pile of horse manure.

Born on the 16th, this lover will appreciate stability and solidity in the relationship, with an occasional splash of doing the unexpected. You will get the most mileage out of little sexy surprises with this lover. You know . . . little sexy notes hung in the shower, or suggestive sketches tucked into a pocket. I doubt if your efforts would be in vain!

Born on the 17th, this lover truly believes in the importance of taking time out for intimacy. However, this is not a relationship that we should allow to run out of steam. Perhaps you may have to be the one to do most of the stoking of romantic fires, at least in the beginning, or at times of stress and fatigue. On the bright side, though, your loving efforts should be more than rewarded!

Born on the 18th, this lover will most likely treat a loving relationship like a sacred cow. When the person born on the 18th is head over heels in love, passion reigns supreme, and he/she will go to the death to protect it. Jealousy and passion are usually the keywords that describe this lover. Definitely worth nurturing, wouldn't you say?

Born on the 19th, this lover greatly respects integrity and loyalty. Flirtations don't sit well with the number 19 birth-date personality. This person requires faith and fidelity, and will probably offer the same. Being true to your word will build a fortress of trust in this relationship. Together, words of love and praise will be a treasured hallmark of this relationship.

Born on the 20th, this lover may be reluctant to spend time, money or effort, until there is a commitment of abiding fidelity. After that, the floodgates may swing wide open, as you experience a plethora of generosity. In return, this lover requires that you think big, open your heart and mind, and express passion. Your imagination has to run wild with this lover, and you have to stay loose!

Born on the 21st, this lover may initially question and challenge your attachment to external values. He/she wants you both to develop your self-confidence, and self-assuredness, without interference from outside influences. Music, art and beauty are integral parts of this relationship. Unselfish love and unconditional giving are primary ingredients of this relationship.

Born on the 22nd, this lover is so busy working hard, that he/she may initially prefer to keep his/her shoulder to the wheel rather than taking time for "wild pony rides." He/she is emotional and feels things deeply, so be aware of the great vulnerability. Words spoken casually to this lover, with the greatest of innocence, can wreak havoc with a sensitive relationship. Think twice before speaking harshly to this lover!

Born on the 23rd, this lover may be so busy traveling, changing his/her residence, and/or finding a new place of employment that you will have to make a pronounced effort to have some time out. This is an impulsive person, who may act before thinking. Strangely enough, the decisions made are usually correct.

The old adage, "Marry in haste, repent at leisure," may apply to this person. Expect fun and a spontaneous relationship with this lover.

Born on the 24th, you can expect this lover to go out of his/her way to always create an aura of harmony and bliss. This is not a person who will take kindly to loud noise, discordant relationships, or a lack of serenity. Ideally, life with a person born on the 24th can pretty much assure you of a home filled with beauty, culture and music. On the negative side, there may be the problem of a refusal to deal with troubling issues.

Born on the 25th, this lover may occasionally be a little on the introspective or brooding side. Perhaps it might be confused with thinking or contemplating. The greater reality, however, might be more of a withdrawal into themselves, or a need for private or personal time. You should not be offended by this, and should recognize that in a short (hopefully!) period of time, he/she will be coming out of the cocoon of privacy, back to having a somewhat normal relationship with you! This lover requires patience and nurturing, but it will pay dividends.

Born on the 26th, this lover enjoys building a base of power and strength, occasionally at the cost of near and dear relationships. His/her priorities won't always seem to be imbedded deeply enough in the relationship. This is a person who definitely needs to burn his/her cell phone and beeper. The secret of success with this person may very well be to prioritize. Make sure that you are on the top of the list of priorities. If not, negotiate!

Born on the 27th, this is a lover who can usually be counted on to be where he/she says he/she will be, and also to do what he/she says he/she will do. This person is usually reliable, honorable and faithful. There may be an occasional touch of extravagance, or impracticality leaching into the relationship. If this occurs, it will be up to you to financially "pull in the reins." This person usually has great taste, and likes the world to know it.

Born on the 28th, this lover may be so entertaining and bright that he/she is a pleasure to be with. Always versatile and imaginative, and seeming to have no limit on creative talents, you may have a run for your money. You may not be able to keep up! The downside is that this person can be wearing and tiresome to you, if you require peace and serenity!

Born on the 29th, this lover is usually on the cutting edge of all new technology, and exciting ideas and concepts. What may not sit well in a relationship is the desire to always be involved with something new or exciting, rather than appreciating what is in their own backyard. This person can grow tiresome because of the unending search for the untried. He/she may need to be reminded that the greatest joys may be right under our noses.

Born on the 30th, you can expect this lover to express his/her creativity in all ways that are pleasing to the soul, including the eye and palate. For example, you may find all of your meals prepared by what seems like a master chef with a great sense of aesthetics. Or at least someone who envisions himself/herself to be. Therein lies the rub . . . his/her reality, or grip on the situation, may not always be all that you would like it to be!

Born on the 31st, this lover may be more hardworking and dedicated to a cause that he/she needs to be. From your perspective, you may see a person who is pouring more energy into a project or situation than he/she needs to. In addition to that, there may be a strong feeling of being neglected on your part. On the bright side, this person wants very much to please those whom he/she loves, and will respond to a request for a more reasonable approach to life.

THE MYSTERY OF THE KABBALAH

Why has the mystery of the Kabbalah survived and been a source of great wisdom for centuries?

Perhaps it is because this mystical Jewish system of interpretation of the Scriptures teaches that every word, letter, number and accent of the Scriptures contains hidden mysteries. It's fascinating to realize the Kabbalah teaches that its signs and writings are used as amulets and in magical practices.

The Kabbalah has two principal written sources. The first, *Sefer Yezira,* which was probably written in the third century, is a series of monologues supposedly delivered by the patriarch Abraham.

The second source, *Zohar,* is a mystical commentary on the *Pentateuch* that was written by Moses de León in the thirteenth century, but attributed to Simon ben Yohai, a great scholar of the second century.

The movement appears to have arisen in the eleventh century in France, and spread mostly to Spain. After the expulsion of the Jews from Spain in 1492, the Kabbalah was considered by many to be a message directly from God. This was especially due to the contributions of Isaac Luria. This form of the Kabbalah had many followers, including the would-be Messiah, Sabatai Zevi. It was also a major influence in the development of eighteenth-century Hasidism.

The Kabbalah is considered by scholars to be one of the earliest combinations of mysticism and numerology. Using a Pythagorean numerical system, the mysteries of the Scriptures were interpreted by followers of the Kabbalistic system. Many students of the Kabbalah have associated its interpretation with the hidden meanings of numbers and letters in the Bible, and with its reports of miraculous acts.

Teachings of the Kabbalah heavily influenced many wisdom schools such as the Rosicrucians, Freemasons, Theosophists, the Golden Dawn, and other systems that taught about the mysteries of life.

Modern Judaic teachings of the Kabbalah include the works of Baal Shem Tov, Eliyahu of Vilna, Shneur Zalman, and Dov Baer.

CELEBRITY BIRTHDAYS

Famous people born on the 1st: Paul Revere, Betsy Ross, Charles Bickford and J. Edgar Hoover.

Famous people born on the 2nd: Sally Rand, Isaac Asimov, Julius LaRosa and Jim Bakker.

Famous people born on the 3rd: J. R. R. Tolkien, Marion Davies, Victor Borge, Dabney Coleman and Victoria Principal.

Famous people born on the 4th: Louis Braille, Tom Thumb, Barbara Rush and Dyan Cannon.

Famous people born on the 5th: George Washington Carver, Robert Duvall, Diane Keaton and Pamela Sue Martin.

Famous people born on the 6th: Carl Sandburg, Tom Mix, Sun Myung Moon and Nancy Lopez.

Famous people born on the 7th: Butterfly McQueen, Charles Addams, William Peter Blatty and Jann Wenner.

Famous people born on the 8th: José Ferrer, Soupy Sales, Elvis Presley and David Bowie.

Famous people born on the 9th: George Balanchine, Richard M. Nixon and Joan Baez.

Famous people born on the 10th: Ray Bolger, Sal Mineo and Rod Stewart.

Famous people born on the 11th: Grant Tinker, Rod Taylor and Ben Crenshaw.

Famous people born on the 12th: Jack London, Howard Stern and Kristie Alley.

Famous people born on the 13th: Sophie Tucker, Robert Stack and Gwen Verdon.

Famous people born on the 14th: Albert Schweitzer, Hal Roach, Cecil Beaton, Andy Rooney and Faye Dunaway.

Famous people born on the 15th: Goodman Ace, Edward Teller, Lloyd Bridges and Chuck Berry.

Famous people born on the 16th: Ethel Merman, Eartha Kitt, Francesco Scavullo and Sade.

Famous people born on the 17th: Noah Beery, Mack Sennett, Al Capone and Betty White.

Famous people born on the 18th: Oliver Hardy, Cary Grant, Danny Kaye and Kevin Costner.

Famous people born on the 19th: Edgar Allan Poe, John Raitt, Jean Stapleton and Dolly Parton.

Famous people born on the 20th: George Burns, Joy Adamson and Edwin Aldrin.

Famous people born on the 21st: Christian Dior, Jack Nicklaus and Mac Davis.

Famous people born on the 22nd: Sam Cooke, John Hurt and Piper Laurie.

Famous people born on the 23rd: Chita Rivera, Princess Caroline and Dan Duryea.

Famous people born on the 24th: Ernest Borgnine, Oral Roberts and Mary Lou Retton.

Famous people born on the 25th: Somerset Maugham, Edwin Newman and Dean Jones.

Famous people born on the 26th: Paul Newman, Jules Feiffer and Eddie Van Halen.

Famous people born on the 27th: Lewis Carroll, Hyman Rickover and Skitch Henderson.

Famous people born on the 28th: Jackson Pollock, Susan Sontag and Alan Alda.

Famous people born on the 29th: W. C. Fields, Tom Selleck and Ann Jillian.

Famous people born on the 30th: Franklin D. Roosevelt, Vanessa Redgrave and Phil Collins.

Famous people born on the 31st: Jackie Robinson, Norman Mailer and Suzanne Pleshette.

WEIGHT LOSS ACCORDING
TO YOUR BIRTH DATE

"He must increase, but I must decrease."

—*The Bible, John 3:30*

Before embarking on any weight-loss program, please check with a professional medical practitioner.

If you were born on:

The 1st: Eat slowly! Your rushing through the day to accomplish all that you need to do will not serve you well during mealtimes. Relax, listen to calming music during meals. Avoid the stimulation and excitement that might come from watching television.

The 2nd: It's not easy, but write down everything you eat. You will probably be surprised at how fast the calories add up! Watch your fat intake. It's not always easy for number 2 people to do without the "extras," which frequently help to pack on pounds. Make sure you exercise or walk daily.

The 3rd: Your meals should be an aesthetic experience. Number 3 people need to experience an almost sensual meal for proper digestion, and ultimate weight loss. If you enjoy what you are eating, and are aware of every mouthful, you will undoubtedly lose weight.

The 4th: Don't skip meals. You know that you will become ravenous, and possibly lose control, just when you need it. Pace yourself, avoid buffets at restaurants and parties. The chances are that one of the keys to weight loss and control is avoiding extreme hunger.

The 5th: You love variety in everything! Meals do not have to be boring to help you lose or control your weight. Make sure that your meals contain a variety of fresh fruits, vegetables and protein. The key to your weight loss is balance, harmony and variety.

The 6th: Eat at regular hours. Some people can live and eat with an erratic schedule, with meals eaten at haphazard times and hours. This does not work well for you. Follow an uncompromising schedule, get your body used to it. Try not to have high calorie snacks in between meals.

The 7th: Don't be fanatical or extreme. Many number 7 people have eating disorders, thanks to their ability to be over-controlled or too disciplined. Don't become too controlled in your weight-loss patterns. The result is that your body will become too efficient, and be able to survive on too few calories without weight loss.

The 8th: Don't forget to take time to eat. Stop working long enough to eat wisely. Don't rush, or eat on the run, simply because you have a heavy work schedule, or are faced with many responsibilities.

The 9th: Don't eat empty calories, or food that will not bring you greater vitality and health. Be aware of what you are eating. We all need the vitality and nutrition that comes from "living" or vital foods. Number 9 people have a tendency to eat devitalized, cooked-out or dead foods. These foods, such as cookies, do not contribute to overall health and weight control.

The 10th: See number 1 birth date.

The 11th: You are a "power" number who, more than most of the other birth dates, needs to depend on building body strength and the burning of calories with metaphysical techniques. That includes regimes such as hatha yoga and meditation, and Qi Gong.

The 12th: See number 3 birth date.

The 13th: See number 4 birth date.

The 14th: See number 5 birth date.

The 15th: See number 6 birth date.

The 16th: See number 7 birth date.

The 17th: See number 8 birth date.

The 18th: See number 9 birth date.

The 19th: See number 1 birth date.

The 20th: See number 2 birth date.

The 21st: See number 3 birth date.

The 22nd: A master number that requires especially great attention to the body-mind-spirit connection for weight loss. Meditation that draws your attention to the peak functioning of your metabolism is the key to your weight loss. Clearly "see" yourself in your mind's eye at what you feel is your perfect weight. Do this before and after all meals.

The 23rd: See number 5 birth date.

The 24th: See number 6 birth date.

The 25th: See number 7 birth date.

The 26th: See number 8 birth date.

The 27th: See number 9 birth date.

The 28th: See number 1 birth date.

The 29th: See number 11 birth date.

The 30th: See number 3 birth date.

The 31st: See number 4 birth date.

For all numbers, remember that steady, permanent weight loss occurs when we perspire and get our heart rates up for fifteen to twenty minutes, a minimum of three times a week. The best overall exercise for weight control and wellness is walking briskly. That doesn't mean shopping!

Chapter 5.

What Day Is This?

Universal and Personal Year,
Month and Day with Characteristics

The universal year is simply the numerological value of any year as it applies, in general, to everyone. For example, if we take the year 1999 and add the four digits together $(1+9+9+9 = 28)$ and reduce that value to a single digit $(2+8 = 10$, and then $1+0 = 1)$, we find that it has a vibration of "one." For the year 2000, it's easy to see that it is a "two" universal year $(2+0+0+0 = 2)$. The year the Titanic sank, 1912 $(1+9+1+2 = 13; 1+3 = 4)$, and the year Germany invaded Poland, 1939 $(1+9+3+9 = 22; 2+2 = 4)$, were both universal "four" years, which is not an easy vibration. Since these yearly influences apply to everyone, they must be taken into account when we determine the personal year vibrations, as will be shown later in this chapter.

UNIVERSAL YEAR CHARACTERISTICS

A "one" universal year has the following nature: New beginnings. Patterns of social behavior, fashion, economics and international relationships, started in this year, will generally extend through the following eight years.

A "two" universal year has the following nature: International relationships such as treaties, signed or broken, harmony, discord, alliances. There will be new companies starting up and old companies going bankrupt. There will be a greater number of both marriages and divorces. There will be new friendships and more attention to the grievances of women.

A "three" universal year has the following nature: Creative expression in the arts and theater will bloom. Public recreation will be at a high point; resorts and beaches will be full and sell-out attendance will be the rule at sporting events and other public displays.

A "four" universal year has the following nature: Hard work will be the rule, for nations as well as for individuals.

A "five" universal year has the following nature: Changes, and a need for flexibility and adaptability in international dealings.

A "six" universal year has the following nature: Adjustments, both war and peace treaties. Like the "two" year, a disproportionately large number of marriages.

A "seven" universal year has the following nature: A spiritual year when people turn more to their religions or their inner spirituality. Restful.

An "eight" universal year has the following nature: International big business and finance will be at the forefront. Currency exchange will be prominent. There is a likelihood of large-scale famine and epidemics.

A "nine" universal year has the following nature: Completion of universal or international projects. There will be increased interest in religion and metaphysics. Church services will be full.

An "eleven" universal year has the following nature: Large building projects, especially for schools and libraries.

A "twenty-two" universal year has the following nature: More large projects to build hospitals, schools, libraries, etc.

THE UNIVERSAL MONTH

The universal month number is found by adding the number of the month to the universal year number. For example, November 1999 is found by adding the number of the month, eleven, to the universal year number of "one" which we determined when we reduced 1999 at the beginning of the chapter. Thus 11+1 = 12, and 1+2 = 3. Therefore, November 1999 has a universal month number of "three." For people in general, this would be a month of creative expression, recreation and enjoyable social events.

THE UNIVERSAL DAY

The universal day number is found by adding the number of the calendar day to the universal month. Continuing with our foregoing example, if we choose the 22nd of the month of November 1999, we would add four (2+2) to the universal month number of "three," which results in a universal day number of "seven." For people in general, this would be a quiet day of introspection or, perhaps, study. As mentioned before, when the effects of the personal year, month or day are determined, we must keep in mind the natures of the prevailing universal year, month and day.

PERSONAL YEAR, MONTH AND DAY

To find the personal year of anyone, simply add the birth month and date together and, to that sum, add the universal year number. For a child born on March 12, 1999, we would add 3+12, which equals 15, and then 1+5, which equals 6, and to this add the universal year number for 1999, which, we know from above, is "one." This equals seven, which is the personal year vibration of the first year for that baby. (Since a "seven" year is a rather quiet one, perhaps the parents will not have their sleep disturbed too often by their newborn.)

Let's take a few other examples and determine the personal year number for the year 2000, which is obviously a "two" universal year.

BIRTHDAY	MONTH#		DAY#		UNIVERSAL YEAR		PERSONAL YEAR
November 2:	11	+	2	+	2	=	15 (1+5) = 6
May 28:	5	+	28	+	2	=	35 (3+5) = 8
September 14:	9	+	14	+	2	=	25 (2+5) = 7
February 25:	2	+	25	+	2	=	29 (2+9)=11 (2)

Note that the fourth example yielded a personal year of "eleven," and that this was not reduced further to two since eleven is a master number which, like twenty-two, is not reduced to a single digit. We understand that they also have the vibrations of a two or a four, as was indicated, but that each is a higher octave, which has some special spiritual characteristics. Notice also, that the full totals were found before reducing to a single digit, so that a master number would not be overlooked. For example, if the third birthday, above, had been June 14, we might have reduced the day of the month (14) to five which, added to 6+2, would have totaled 13, which would reduce (1+3) to four. Actually, the total would be 6+14+2 = 22, the higher octave of four, a master number. As will be seen in the following list of personal year characteristics, an "eleven" or "twenty-two" personal year has a greater significance than a "two" or a "four." Remember, when evaluating the effect of the personal year, also consider the universal year number since this will affect the individual as well, but to a lesser degree.

SIGNIFICANCE OF PERSONAL YEARS

Number "One" Personal Year: A New Start

This is the beginning of a new nine-year cycle. It's the year to set the standard and the pace for whatever you wish to accomplish during the succeeding eight years. Your personal vibrations are strong in this year. It's the year to start new endeavors. Don't hold back. Use your initiative. Assert your opinions and willpower. Full steam ahead! You may have to go it alone, but there will be less interference with your actions this year. However, you must avoid arrogance and any tendency to ride roughshod over others. You will likely encounter major changes in your life such as moving into a new home or starting a new job or career. This is the year to accept change. Travel is likely this year, as is the prospect of forming lasting friendships, both socially and in business. Put forth your creative ideas and expect gratifying results. The "one" year is under the rulership of the sun; you should "shine" this year.

Number "Two" Personal Year: Teamwork

This is a year to form partnerships, personal or business, or to work cooperatively with others. Contrary to the number "one" personal year, this is a time to control your will and exuberance toward the end of working well with others. You must accept the ideas of others as being on an equal basis with your own. This is a year for new friendships and, very commonly, for both marriages and divorces. Since it is not a year to strike out on your own, accept help and guidance from others as you go through this period. Your personal magnetism this year will attract people to you, and that can lead to rewarding personal or business relationships. However, exercise discrimination and be patient. Under the emotional, sensitive and traditional nature of the moon, this is a year to work out the details rather than to start large, new projects that would meet with feelings of apprehension in others.

Number "Three" Personal Year: Enjoyment

This year, under the influence of the planet Jupiter, should be a very happy time. This is a year for self-expression in art, music, writing, etc. Push creativity to the forefront. Like the "one" year, this is an excellent time to put forth your ideas. Social vibrations are very high this year. Friendships should bloom and it's a good year for business if you keep it on a light, friendly and sociable level. It's a good year for joining a club or organization for either personal satisfaction or business advantage. The vibration of this year can lead to scattering of energy, talents or assets, and this should be guarded against. Be careful about what you put in writing or to what you sign your name. However, whatever you write this year, a book, screenplay, drama, etc., should be especially marketable. This is a good year for innovative marketing and merchandising.

Number "Four" Personal Year: Work

The negative polarity of the Sun interacting with the Earth keeps our feet on the ground in this year. This is a nose-to-the-grindstone sort of year. It's very unlikely that you would be able to make a significant change in career or lifestyle. Whatever your starting situation might be in this year will be likely to continue to the year's end. It's like being slotted to move along a particular path, and it's very difficult to jump out of the groove. It's important to work hard and be mindful of details. It could be a year of loss and hard times if we don't tend to business in a "four" year. This is a year for building upon what you have and laying a solid foundation for your future financial standing. This is a good year for solidifying relationships, especially in the family. Basically, it's more a year for character development than for material gain or fun and games.

Number "Five" Personal Year: Adaptability/Change

Be prepared to innovate, to come up with new ideas to improve business, career or personal relationships. Prepare also to accept change when it comes in this "five" year, under the rulership of the planet Mercury. Changes of dwelling place are typical of this year. Renovation and refurbishment are also typical. Travel, for business or pleasure, is likely, as are new relationships. Take that vacation trip you've been looking to as a reward for work done in the previous "four" year. Watch out for extramarital affairs if you're married. Things started this year may not be permanent, however, like the "three" year. The use of words will be influential. It's a good time for writing, teaching, lecturing, drama and all media involvement. Your intellect will be especially sharp this year, and your mind will be open to new knowledge and understanding.

Number "Six" Personal Year: Responsibility

Under the nurturing influence of Venus, this is a year to make sure everything is organized and businesslike. Debts should be paid and collected or, at least, arrangements made for the payments or collections of debts. Like the "two" year, this is a likely year for marriages or divorces. For a marriage in this year, make sure that the domestic life is worked out equitably to the satisfaction of both parties. This should lead to a harmonious and happy relationship. The urge in the "five" year, for change of dwelling place, would best be satisfied with the actual transaction and move in this "six" year. Domestic matters, in general, will be in the forefront this year and new responsibilities may have to be shouldered, whether balancing the budget, refurbishing the home or providing for family needs. This should work out this year, resulting in surroundings with increased harmony and beauty. Since number "six" relates to the law of supply, there should be ample provision for, at least, all immediate needs.

Number "Seven" Personal Year:
Personal Recharging

Under the mystical and spiritual vibrations of the moon and Neptune, this is a good year for personal recuperation, introspection, study, and self-improvement. It's a great year for a sabbatical. This is a bad year for anything of a material nature, so don't start a new business, job or investment. Rather, take the time to see where you are and do some soul-searching as to where you'd like to be. Lay the plans that you will implement in the next year. The exception to the foregoing is anything that lies at a distance, since unexpected benefit may come from that quarter. Also, keep up correspondence with friends or relatives who live far away. It's a good year to take courses of study for your business or career or just for personal satisfaction or self-improvement. You may find that meditation, mysticism and spiritual development hold strong attraction for you this year. This is an excellent time to delve into these areas and develop your intuitive powers. Don't worry if you experience lack of energy this year, since it's only temporary. If you are looking for a new career or business this year, pursue travel or communications.

Number "Eight" Personal Year: Finances

The no-nonsense energies of Saturn impact the Earth in an "eight" year. With an upswing of energy and power within you, this is the year for pursuit of material things, of money. Proceed carefully so as not to incur loss, but this is the time to invest, expand your business and to take any suitable opportunity that presents itself to increase your wealth. Both big business and philanthropy are ruled by number "eight," so conduct your activities to benefit others, as well as yourself. Your executive powers should be at a peak this year, enabling you to command any situation. Ethical conduct and humanitarian activities are the counterbalances needed to insure success and gain in the material arena.

Number "Nine" Personal Year: Completion/Termination

The powerful energy of Mars, this year, is for wrapping up, not initiating; for harvesting, not sowing. This is not a good year to start new projects, jobs or relationships. Anything started this year is not likely to continue. This is a year to take care of loose ends and unfinished business, including your personal health and fitness considerations. Clear the decks for the new nine-year cycle that starts with the following number "one" year. This is a year to get rid of things, associations or relationships that are not in your best interests. However, it is best not to change your job this year, since the income from that endeavor could come to an end. This is not an easy year. There could be loss and even ruin if the preceding years of the cycle have not been lived in a positive manner. In general, this is a year for a variety of involvements or experiences. Perhaps the most important is that of a growing interest in the occult, with an attendant increase of intuition and psychic ability. Rely upon your impressions. Be satisfied with your accomplishment of the closing nine-year cycle, and look forward with optimism and understanding to the new cycle.

Number "Eleven" Personal Year: Idealism

The 84 year orbit of Uranus relates to the normal human life-span. It influences us to think beyond everyday considerations. This higher octave of the "two" year is definitely not a good time for material gain and the acquisition of wealth. It is a good year for personal development in spirituality, arts and writing. Like the "seven" year, it's a time for introspection and inspiration. Put your highest concepts and ideals into practice. Be a teacher or example-setter for others.

Number "Twenty-two" Personal Year: Altruism

As in the "two" year the Moon increases sensitivity and consideration of others. This higher octave of the "four" year is similar to the "eleven" year, but to an even greater degree. It's a very poor year for personal gain. Any undertakings should be for the purpose of benefiting people in general. Public service is the order of the year.

THE PERSONAL MONTH

The personal month is found by adding the number of the month being considered to the number of the personal year. For example, for the month of November (an 11), if a person is in a number "five" personal year, then 11+5 = 16; 1+6 = 7. It is a "seven" personal month. Here are some more examples. For the month of March in a "nine" personal year, add 3+9 = 12; 1+2 = 3 (a "three" personal month). For the month of July in a "three" personal year, add 7+3 = 10; 1+0 = 1 (a "one" personal month).

The characteristics of the personal months are very much the same as the personal years.

Personal Months

1. This is a busy month for you. It's a time to use your original ideas to start new projects or to modify or enlarge what is already in existence. Your leadership is important this month; this is not a time to play second fiddle.

2. Teamwork is the keyword this month. Cooperate with others, in business or on a personal level. Compromise, if needed, to keep things on an even keel, without disruption.

3. Don't hide your talent under a bushel this month. Express your creativity, use your communication skills. This is a great month for enjoying social activities and making new friends.

4. This is a month for work. Be practical and productive. Take care of all the little details and proceed in an organized manner. Put matters on a sound footing this month.

5. Be prepared for changes this month. Be adaptable and open for new ideas, new projects and new people. Travel may be in store for you this month.

6. It is a time to face up to any responsibilities that may have been neglected, especially regarding home and family. A time for redecorating or refurbishing your surroundings. This is a common month for marriage or divorce.

7. Research, study, analyze, look within, renew your spiritual connections. It's a time to gain knowledge, formulate plans and patiently await the opportune time to act.

8. A good month for business opportunities. Move forward into new areas or engage in expansion of current activities based upon sound financial judgment and prudent management.

9. This is a month for service to others, and to put humanitarian issues first. It is also a time to take care of loose ends that are hanging over from the past eight months.

11. A time for personal inspiration and spiritual insight. A time to teach or to help others, particularly in the area of spiritual awareness and knowledge. Also a time for new ideas or inventions.

22. This is the time to think big for the benefit of humanity, to put personal concerns aside and to be involved in major projects for the betterment of people in general.

THE PERSONAL DAY

The personal day is found by adding the number of the calendar day to the personal month number. For example, if the individual in the first example above who is in a "five" personal year and who has determined that November of that year is a "seven" personal month for him/her, wishes to know what kind of a day the 17th of that month (November) would be, he/she simply adds the personal month number, "seven," to the day of the month (seventeen). Thus, 7+17 = 24; 2+4 = 6. It is, therefore, a "six" personal day, with a vibration that benefits domestic involvement.

PERSONAL DAYS

A "one" personal day: Initiate action. Make appointments and work out business deals.

A "two" personal day: Engage in cooperative ventures. It's

good for agreements and associations. A day for personal relationships, also.

A "three" personal day: Best for communication, socializing and self-expression. Artistic involvement is best on this day.

A "four" personal day: Work hard. Be productive.

A "five" personal day: Good for travel and contacting people, including advertising. Make any planned changes today.

A "six" personal day: A good day for anything relating to the home, such as house or apartment hunting, shopping for furniture, etc.

A "seven" personal day: A good day for rest, study, meditation and spiritual pursuits. Good also for family activities.

An "eight" personal day: Good for any material or financial involvements.

A "nine" personal day: For finishing projects already started. Not good for making new plans or starting new projects.

Note: The master numbers "eleven" and "twenty-two" are not used for personal days since their scope is too great to be assigned to a single day. Any of the nine personal days may be involved in working toward the goal of accomplishment in the areas of the master numbers.

Chapter 6.

....

By the Numbers! – Life Cycles

We will now work with the full birth date to determine the life path and the three life cycles or sub-paths.

We will use a hypothetical young man with a birth date of February 25, 1965. To find the numerological value of the full birth date, we add the month, day and year numbers as follows: 2+25+1965

This totals 1992. We then add 1+9+9+2, which equals 21. (Remember, find the full total before reducing it so you don't miss a master number like eleven or twenty-two. If the forgoing example had been one number higher, we would have had a twenty-two master number.) The value of 21 reduces to 2+1 = 3. This "three" life path denotes a life of creativity, artistic endeavors, communication, social activity and much enjoyment of life through a number of recreational activities.

LIFE PATH DESCRIPTIONS

A "One" Life Path—Initiative

This path calls for a life of positive action resulting in achievement. This will be a path of originality, ambition, self-confidence, and creativity. The person upon this path will be self-reliant and prefers to go it alone rather than be in a cooperative venture with partners or within a group. Individuality is a keyword. This will most likely be a very full and active life. CAUTION: A person on this path must learn to make his or her own decisions and not settle into the norm that satisfies others. Do not neglect development of the inner, spiritual self. Guard against arrogance, egotism, selfishness and being domineering to others. Learn to get along.

A "Two" Life Path—Cooperation

People on this path work well with others, as partners or in group situations. They are good at work requiring attention to detail. There is a desire for companionship and love; these people almost always marry since home and family are so important. This is the path of the conservative peacemaker who is thoughtful to others, and who reaches success mainly through working with and being helpful to others. CAUTION: Guard against being subservient to others to the point of becoming a doormat. Avoid being overly shy or sensitive and putting yourself down in deference to others. Cultivate your willpower and ability to step out and take risks.

A "Three" Life Path—Enjoyment

This is a path of creative self-expression, particularly in the arts or some form of communication. This is the path of social activities with lots of friends and associates. These people are originators of many creative ideas and concepts, and are often writers, actors, singers or public speakers. They love to enjoy life and beauty, and may be a bit unrestrained in sexual activities. Creativity, talent, originality, optimism, imagination, intuition, beauty and joy are aspects of this life path. CAUTION: A person on this path must develop self-expression. Avoid jealousy, criticism, impatience and intolerance.

A "Four" Life Path—Practical

This is the path of hard work and effort. This path develops traits of organization, loyalty, responsibility and trust. These productive people usually have a happy home and family life, and a good job or successful business. They frequently are pillars of their community and the foundation of our economy. They are thorough, methodical and organized in their work and very detail-oriented. They adjust well to routine. CAUTION: Avoid being a complete workaholic and take time to enjoy life and get out of your rut. Learn to socialize, converse and relate to others. Show them that you are not dull.

A "Five" Life Path—Freedom

Frequent changes are in store. This may be difficult at times, but not dull. Travel as well as variety is very likely for the individual on this path. In all probability there will be adventure, curiosity and freedom. People upon this path are restless, impatient, quick-witted and active; they do not usually form permanent attachments with others. They are great in social circumstances and deal well with people. Since they find routine boring and like to try new things frequently, they are apt to scatter their energies. They have to guard against lack of responsibility, inconsideration and overindulgence in sex, alcohol or other substances.

A "Six" Life Path—Responsibility

This path usually leads to success through service and responsibility. These people must be open to making adjustments, decisions and playing the role of peacemaker. This is especially true with regard to home and family, which are of utmost importance to them. Help to others should be given freely, with no self-interest involved. Individuals on this path love a peaceful, comfortable, beautiful environment with music being an essential part. These humanitarian people are often doctors, teachers or in some way involved with the community. They must guard against being stubborn, unreasonable, meddlesome or demanding of others.

A "Seven" Life Path—Knowledge

This is the path of the philosopher, visionary and deep thinker who craves peace, spirituality and wisdom. These people love to read, study and explore, preferring a restful, peaceful life to material return. They are fascinated by mysteries of the metaphysical world and are good professors or doctors as well as priests, rabbis or ministers. These individuals are usually loners who aren't the best marriage material and don't make friends easily. They have good powers of observation and very analytical minds that make them excellent in positions of research or invention. They should guard against indifference, secretiveness, laziness, depression and alcohol abuse.

An "Eight" Life Path—Material

These are the achievers who are on a path of material gain, authority and financial success. Although these individuals have great inner strength and courage, they are also generous and dependable. They generally possess good judgment, ambition and courage, and choose not to follow an easy path, but strive, with determination, for success. They usually wind up as executives in finance, transportation, shipping, education or in a successful business of their own. It is important for them to balance this drive for success with spirituality in order to reach true success. They should guard against intolerance, abuse of power, and being a workaholic to the detriment of home and family.

A "Nine" Life Path—Understanding

People on this path are usually compassionate and understanding, and lean toward a life of humanitarian service. This is also, we believe, a path that encompasses all the other paths as sort of a review prior to stepping up to a new cycle of soul development. These individuals are frequently world travelers who are intuitive and knowledgeable. They are usually in successful marriages due to their kind and considerate natures. Their greatest success comes through selfless service to others, usually in some sort of charity, hospital or nonprofit organization. They must guard against being moody, miserly, selfish, unkind or timid.

An "Eleven" Life Path—Inspiration

The path of this master number involves intuition, idealism and even revelation. For those not ready for this path, the lower octave of "two" will apply. For those able to handle it, there is a great responsibility to mankind that usually involves being before the public as a diplomat, lecturer, minister, or spiritual leader. These idealistic, intelligent people reach success through inspiration and leadership for others. They pass on to others what has been revealed to them and set a good example with their personal lives. They are also found to be artists, writers, healers, teachers, scientists, psychologists and mediators. This is not the best individual for a personal relationship due to the universal outlook. These people must guard against selfishness, egotism, indifference and lack of purpose.

A "Twenty-two" Life Path—Universal

Like the "eleven," this path is for advanced souls. For those not ready for it, the lower octave "four" life path will apply. The "twenty-two" master number life path requires a universal outlook that will benefit mankind. The individuals on this path who are generally honest, sincere and truthful have an outlook of much larger scope than the everyday tasks and circumstances of life. They are known as master builders who are involved with large construction projects or humanitarian programs; often on an international level. They are often architects, engineers, statesmen, university professors or public benefactors. They are leaders who put humanitarian concerns ahead of personal considerations. It is not an easy path. They must guard against self-promotion, desire for quick financial gain, egotism, indifference and mental or emotional tension.

THE THREE LIFE CYCLES OR SUB-PATHS

Overall, life can be broken down into three cycles or sub-paths, usually called the formative, productive and harvest periods. These three cycles begin at birth and approximately at ages twenty-eight and fifty-seven. This is an example of how closely numerology is related to astrology. The length of these periods is partly due to the eighty-four-year orbit of Uranus being considered the span of a normal lifetime, and partly to a twenty-eight year, four month cycle of revolutions of the moon. There is some difference of opinion on the exact year of changing from one cycle to the next, but I believe that the most credible authorities consider it to be as follows: The second cycle begins with the start of the number "one" year that is closest to the twenty-eighth birthday. The third cycle begins with the start of the number "one" year closest to the fifty-seventh birthday.

Using the same February 25, 1965 birthday as above, for the life-path determination, we now find the three separate values of the birth date. For the month, we, of course, have 2. For the day of the month (25), we add $2+5 = 7$. For the year, we add $1+9+6+5 = 21; 2+1 = 3$.

For the time when these cycles begin, using the month and day, which we add together ($2+25 = 27, 2+7 = 9$) and reduce to nine, and add that to the universal year number when born (1965

= 1+9+6+5 = 21, 2+1 = 3) which is three. The sum of 9 and 3 is 12, which reduces (1+2) to 3. Therefore, this individual, born 2/25/65, was in a "three" personal year when born. Twenty-seven years later (three cycles of nine years) he was also in a "three" personal year. Two years earlier, he would have been in a "one" personal year. Therefore his second (productive) cycle started at the age of twenty-five, in 1990, although the full effects would not be felt until the age of twenty-eight (twenty-eight years, four months, to be exact.) Going forward three nine-year cycles, or twenty-seven years, a "one" personal year will occur in 2017, at the age of fifty-two. This is five years before the fifty-seventh birthday, therefore the third (harvest) cycle will not begin until the "one" personal year four years after the fifty-seventh birthday (in 2022), which would be in 2026. There would be a phasing-in during the cusp period starting in 2022, with the full effects in place in 2026.

Therefore: First (Formative) Cycle is "TWO"
                 Second (Productive) Cycle is "SEVEN" at
                    age twenty-five (1990)
                 Third (Harvest) Cycle is "THREE" at age
                    sixty-one (2026)

The first cycle, with a "two" vibration, indicates a time when relationships are very important, whether they involve family, friends, teammates, employers, business partners or sweethearts. The middle cycle is one where study, introspection, and searching for one's place and purpose in the universe would be a continual quest. The third cycle denotes creativity, enjoyment, and involvement in artistic activities or communication of some sort, as well as social activity.

LIFE CYCLE (SUB-PATH) INTERPRETATIONS

A "ONE" Sub-Path

FORMATIVE   This is not an easy cycle, since the individuality is in its formative stage and wants independence but, of course, must be controlled to a point by the parent(s). The child is learning to rely upon its own resources and should be given a reasonable degree of free rein by its parents. Self-confidence, originality, determination and creativity should be encouraged. This person would be likely to go into business for himself or herself at an early age, since he or she would much prefer to be in the driver's seat. The individual should guard against stubbornness and should keep the ego in check in order to get along with others if success is to be achieved.

PRODUCTIVE   Drive, ambition, achievement and success are the keywords. If these individuals are not already in business for themselves, they should be, or they should strive for a managerial or executive position since they are much better at directing others than taking orders. (Unless they're in sales!) Their originality and self-reliance can lead them to the top of their organization. A mundane, dull situation is not for them. Again, keep the ego in check, cultivate patience and understanding; don't ride roughshod over your associates, friends or family.

HARVEST   Due to the great energy of this ("ONE") number, a quiet retirement is not likely. There will probably be much activity for many years after the normal retirement age. If early retirement is presented, the individual will probably start another career or business. If not already involved in the following, these are possible areas that would be fitting, even in later life: executive, manager, inventor, engineer, designer or any position where independent, original thinking and leadership are required.

A "TWO" Sub-Path

✓

FORMATIVE   The inference of this path is that the mother was or will be a much stronger influence on the child than the father, possibly due to divorce or widowhood. Care must be exercised that the child is not spoiled during this emotional period. This period requires training in cooperative effort, harmony, sensitivity to the feelings of others, attention to detail and adaptability, which will all lead to success. There is likely to be artistic or musical talent; excessive shyness and development of an inferiority complex must be guarded against. This is a time for friends and associates; usually partnership and/or marriage will happen before the end of this cycle.

PRODUCTIVE   This is a period for cooperative ventures, teamwork, harmonious associations or partnership. Don't be insensitive to others or forget to pay attention to details, which you normally do so well. Emotional extremes should be controlled; difficulties with partnerships or marriage could occur. Cultivate your natural charm and friendliness toward others; they will want to work with you and please you. Engage in spiritual development as you are inclined, especially your natural healing ability. If you develop psychic ability, don't let it go to your head (in the ego sense).

HARVEST   For most "TWOs" this is a retirement time, with your mate, engaging in enjoyable pursuits such as collecting and socializing in a loving and comfortable environment.

A "THREE" Sub-Path

FORMATIVE   This should be a very pleasant time for a child, with opportunities for self-expression in school plays, music or dance recitals, and in art. A wise parent will support this child's desire for expression. Writing ability may develop fairly early in life and should be especially encouraged. Friends are plentiful and social activities reach a peak at the end of this cycle, in the early twenties. Friends and associates can be very important to the success of these individuals. These people must guard against being a prima donna who sulks when lacking attention, or being jealous or over-emotional.

PRODUCTIVE   This should be the best of the best. It would normally be an easy life with enjoyable work involving self-expression, loving family, many friends and social activities. If creative expression is not satisfied through work, then there will be much expression as an avocation in art, music, writing or painting. These individuals, who are honest, sincere and optimistic, should certainly strive to develop their talents in the arts, designing, decoration or communication to a professional level. Other suitable areas for income would be real estate or stocks and bonds. Guard against extravagance.

HARVEST   This period should be pretty much the same as before, with opportunity for self-expression, family, friends and social activities. These individuals may wish to cut back on socializing to allow more time for expression in the arts, especially writing, since this is a very suitable time to write one or more books, plays or musical compositions.

A "FOUR" Sub-Path

Bern · 27

FORMATIVE This path is very much the opposite of the "THREE" cycles. This is a path of work and application. For a child it would involve application to one's schoolwork, which could come hard, as well as doing household chores. There may be restriction for the child in this life. The lessons to be learned include order, routine, punctuality, follow-through and application of self to work. Life will revolve around what is practical and serviceable. The individual may have to start earning an income early in life due to the family situation. Dreaming is allowed, but only if there is a practical application.

Bern. 52 yr. ✓

PRODUCTIVE The stable foundation started in the formative period is put to use here with continued development of the practical skills of order, hard work and productivity. There will be little time or inclination for travel or carefree living. Creative ideas should be put into practical form. These people are builders, contractors, and business owners, or they could be in science, art or spiritual avenues. They must guard against being workaholics who don't spend enough time with their families or take time to enjoy life.

HARVEST In most cases, work continues into this cycle, whether by necessity or by choice. In many cases it's because the individual has his or her own business, with no inclination to give it up. Or it may be that the person is in an executive position and too valuable to the organization for them to force retirement, while the individual is too much of a workhorse to choose to retire. This is the period when more time should be taken off to enjoy the peaceful comfort of home and family or the enjoyable company of your few special friends.

A *"FIVE" Sub-Path*

FORMATIVE   This path entails change and freedom. It is a relatively carefree cycle, except that there may be some illicit sexual activity. The parents need to set rules and provide guidance without too severely curtailing the child's freedom, while the child must learn the proper use of freedom, not using it to escape from responsibilities and routine. These impulsive individuals are active, restless and curious, always on the lookout for something new and exciting, to the detriment of finishing what they've started. They will probably experience a number of changes of address by the time they reach their teen years, and this may leave them a bit insecure and unsettled. They may go through many jobs while still in this first cycle.

PRODUCTIVE   Travel and frequent changes involving new acquaintances, friends and activities will be the norm in this "FIVE" cycle. In order to progress on this sub-path, the individual must be willing to adapt, to relinquish the old and outmoded, to embrace the new. It is not unusual for major or complete changes in one's life to occur as frequently as every year to year and a half. As changeable as your life is, it not wise to give in to your restless nature and engage in change just for the sake of change. Many opportunities will be presented, so plan and choose wisely. When you make a decision, proceed with purpose, determination and responsibility. Guard against a tendency toward alcohol and gambling. Typical occupations are in the travel industry, investments, legal, sales, advertising, transportation, investigation and communications.

HARVEST   People on this path are not prone to retire. They like an active life involving a lot of moving around and contact with people. If they do leave their jobs or businesses, they will be happy only if their lives contain many new activities, friends, interests, and travel. They like to keep up with the world, keep informed, entertained and continue their education and exposure to new things.

A "SIX" Sub-Path

FORMATIVE   This is the path of responsibility, and early childhood will be likely to have its share. There will probably be many chores, duties and obligations. The parent or parents would be well advised to avoid overloading the youngster with too many tasks, since what is normally a restrictive childhood should not be made intolerable. Many individuals on this path gladly shoulder jobs and responsibility, often due to a needy family member. In many cases the burden is at least partly lifted by the age of twenty and the young man or woman marries early.

PRODUCTIVE   This individual, with a nature of shouldering responsibility and being of service, enjoys working with others, often in jobs to do with home, community, education or institutions. Other typical occupations are as a healer, welfare worker, gardener, chef, lawyer, speaker, singer or rancher. Success, including financial return, is gained through being true to your nature of accepting responsibility and helping others. Marriage is likely, if not already married, and a happy home life is quite common if certain adjustments are made, which may be required due to family responsibilities. These generous and sympathetic people are often perfectionists and require order and beauty in their homes. They should guard against being too charitable to those who don't deserve it and being too demanding of those in their own family.

HARVEST   Although a cycle of a secure nature, responsibilities and restrictions are likely to be part of it. Adjustments should be made and these should be accepted good-naturedly since they will contribute to the development and overall success of the individual. No good deeds are done without reward. If the individual has not yet married, this period would be a good time for it with its rewards of mutual love and affection. It is likely that a beautiful, comfortable home and surroundings exists, since these people are into landscaping, gardening and decorating.

A "SEVEN" Sub-Path

FORMATIVE   A child on this path will be an introvert, seemingly complete within himself or herself. It would be well for the parents to draw the youngster out with conversation and social activity. As the individual grows into adolescence, there will be searching for knowledge, self-purpose and philosophical wisdom. Naturally, this person will be misunderstood and even resented by other youngsters due to the lack of sociability and the apparent independent nature. These are the natural students of the world and they are seldom without a book. They often are attracted to scientific and metaphysical studies. Their quest for knowledge should be encouraged; productivity can come later.

PRODUCTIVE   This is not a cycle for a go-getter, set-the-world-on-fire type of person. It is a peaceful, developmental period, for learning, strengthening spiritual connections, and building faith. The individual will most likely work alone, which is to his or her advantage, and not be disposed toward marriage if that has not already occurred. Opportunities will seem to materialize without being sought. The most likely occupations are in areas requiring research and analysis, in science or inventing. Teaching is very suitable, especially at college level, as is writing of a technical, scientific or metaphysical nature.

HARVEST   Retirement or semiretirement is likely, with continued study, research and writing from a home study. It would be an especially peaceful and quiet time with little activity or socializing, but great progress toward knowledge and wisdom. Marriage is not likely if the person is not already married, but there would probably be a small circle of friends with similar interests. The study of religions, metaphysics or of spiritual subjects would be especially suitable at this time.

An "EIGHT" Sub-Path

FORMATIVE   This is a strong cycle for a child. Parents should not be too generous with money at this time unless guidance is given and followed. These individuals should be taught good judgment in financial matters at an early age. They need to establish a solid foundation of good judgment, ambition and ethical principles. These individuals could go into business at an early age, possibly due to financial need of the family. They would probably be better off working in a group situation and should be careful about putting too much trust in others.

PRODUCTIVE   This cycle relates to great progress in the material; money, finance and big business. With good judgment, it leads to big business, power and accumulation of wealth. There is a strong inner drive that pushes these individuals to positions of power and wealth. It is a time for ambition, achievement, recognition and authority. Success could come through property management or directing a business of your own, since you do best as a leader rather than a follower. The ability to manage money is of prime importance to your success. These individuals must keep in mind that supply comes from a universal source and is for the use of all people. A selfish, grasping attitude toward material gain could throw one off the path of success.

HARVEST   This is not a cycle that engenders retirement. Continued activity is indicated, which with proper application and decision leads to success, money and power. The individual in this cycle is usually the owner of a business or a top executive in an organization. Further hard work and money management is required since this could be an expensive period. Participation in social activities involving clubs and other organizations will bring new friends. Guard against placing trust in the wrong person(s). Study of mystical or spiritual subjects, religion or philosophy would be an ideal way to round out this cycle.

A "NINE" Sub-Path

FORMATIVE   A difficult path for a child, this cycle exerts pressure upon the individual for high performance without equivalent recognition. Fortunately it usually involves good educational opportunities. The "NINE" path encompasses all others and is hard to adjust to. It can cause the individual to be nervous, emotional and fearful. Parents should provide understanding and love. This is a rewarding cycle, in the long run, as the individual develops compassion, understanding, tolerance and service to others. The "NINE" path is that of the humanitarian.

PRODUCTIVE   This is a spiritual path, but with potential for success, especially in public life. It is not a good cycle for marriage since it engenders a state of all-encompassing love rather than individual love. It is also felt that a degree of freedom is required to utilize the full potential of the cycle, which could be virtually limitless with a strong effort. However, success on this path involves unselfish service to humanity. It requires understanding, compassion and selfless service. There can be many highs and lows during this cycle, but great rewards in the long run.

HARVEST   It is typical that the individual in this cycle would be giving inspiration to others through art or writing and personal example. Retirement will probably include involvement in art, drama and philosophy. It will be a time of learning and development. There would likely be charitable work in hospitals and other nonprofit institutions. This is a time to utilize all of one's talents for the betterment of mankind.

An "ELEVEN" Sub-Path

FORMATIVE   This master number cycle is too advanced for all but a few children, so they will travel the lower-octave path of "TWO." This cycle involves inspiring others through science or art. It involves spiritual leadership engendered by inspiration and revelation. These individuals sometimes have psychic abilities and often become psychologists, teachers or philosophers. They must restrict their personal ambitions for the benefit of all.

PRODUCTIVE   People on this path are properly involved with spiritual development rather than material areas. They seem to be driven by an inner purpose to pass on knowledge and inspiration to others. They are often occupied as writers, teachers, ministers, psychics, inventors, charity workers, artists or scientists. They could also be healers or health practitioners. Remember that this path may be too difficult for many. Use the lower-octave "TWO" path in that case.

HARVEST   Retirement is usually engaged in this cycle, but it generally involves continuation of inspired study and, probably, writing about the mystical and spiritual. Frequently the individual is called out into public life due to his or her wisdom and inspiration to others. Again, check the "TWO" pathway.

A "TWENTY-TWO" Sub-Path

FORMATIVE   There is no formative cycle since there is no twenty-second month. The aspects of this path are beyond the capabilities of any child or young person, in any case.

PRODUCTIVE   This is a time of prominence and great attainments. It is the path of the master builder in the form of an architect, engineer or entrepreneur engaged in providing large public structures or programs. These people are also occupied as diplomats and international leaders. They have universal outlook and strive to provide benefit for all of mankind. They successfully combine the material with the spiritual. Again, this is not the path of many; refer to the lower octave path of "FOUR."

HARVEST   These people are usually active throughout this cycle. These individuals may be directors of large organizations, diplomats or public benefactors. They usually engage in religious or spiritual practices such as meditation, yoga or Tai Chi to offset the tremendous stress sometimes imposed upon them. They feel a responsibility for all of mankind. Since this is not a cycle for which many would be suitable, refer to the lower octave path of "FOUR."

Chapter 7.

Numerology of the Name and Alphabet Values

In modern numerology, each letter of the English alphabet has a numerological value or vibration from one to nine. Since there are twenty-six letters in the alphabet, the same number is shared by two or (mostly) three letters. The relationship is shown by the following simple layout.

LETTER VALUES

1	2	3	4	5	6	7	8	9
A	B	C	D	E	F	G	H	I
J	(K)	L	M	N	O	P	Q	R
S	T	U	(V)	W	X	Y	Z	

Note that some authorities assign the master number values of 11 to K and 22 to V. It's been our experience that use of 11 or 22 rarely makes any difference in the final numerological result. For beginners, we suggest you just use the values of one through nine as arrayed above the letters in the foregoing table. In the case of a very short name, the use of 11 or 22 might cause the master numbers 22 or 33* to come up in the final sum. This can be checked out by adding nine (in the case of a K) or by adding eighteen (in the case of a V) to the resulting sum obtained by using just 1 through 9. If an eleven or twenty-two is obtained, then write that number as well as the result after reduction separated by a slash. (For example, 11/2 or 22/4.)

It's a good idea to memorize the numerical values of the letters in the above table. Take one group at a time, like A, J & S with a "one" value, each day or each week and, whenever you think of it, recall the letters to mind for that particular numerological value. I use words or abbreviations for each group to help me recall them to mind. For example, FOX for number "six" is obvious, and "clue" for CLU for number "three" is easy. For "two," I think of BKT being an abbreviation of "book it" or "booklet." ENW for number "five" is like the word "enow," used so often in poetry. DMV ("four") reminds me of the term DMZ ("Demilitarized Zone") so often in the news at the close of the Korean War. For number "eight," the number of executive authority, I perceive HQZ being very much like HQS, a possible abbreviation for "headquarters." For number "nine," the only numeral with just two letters, I think of IR being the abbreviation for infrared, the wavelength at the long-wave end of the visible

---

*Some numerologists consider "thirty-three" a master number. Many respected authorities do not include it. It is not considered a master number for our purposes within this work.

light spectrum. For some letter groups it's difficult to form an association; perhaps rote memory is the only way.

ANALYSIS OF THE NAME—
VOWELS AND CONSONANTS

It is generally agreed that the given name at birth is predominant, and should always be evaluated to determine the basic nature of the individual. The married name, in the case of a woman, or a professional name or some other version of the name, should likewise be evaluated as the nature that is also expressed at this stage in life.

A person's name is broken down in three ways. The numerological value of the *vowels* is determined. The value of the *consonants* is found. The value of *all letters*, which is the sum of the values for vowels and consonants, is determined as well.

The characteristic relating to the vowels is called the Inner Urge or Motivation. It is also known as the heart's desire, secret ambition, or soul urge. It has to do with the person's ideals, deepest desires, hopes, dreams, longings, and hidden likes and dislikes.

That relating to the consonants is called the Inner Self or Impression. It is also known as the appearance, personality, quiet self or passive self. It has to do with one's influence and impression on others, and the inner, motivating force that helps us reach our goals.

The numerological total of all letters in the name is called the Outer Self or Expression. It is also known as the true will, natural talents or abilities. It has to do with one's conduct in the world, what we express to others and what we have to work with.

Use Worksheet No. 1 found in Appendix #2. We suggest you

make a master copy of each of the worksheets on an enlarging copier adjusted so that each format will just fill an 8½-by-11-inch sheet. Then these full-size masters can be used to make same-size copies on any copier, as needed. Print the full name (we suggest using all capital letters) in the blank spaces provided for the first, middle and last names. Try to keep an even spacing of the letters.

If any part of the name is extremely long, or if there are more than three parts of the name, use a second sheet alongside of the first, rather than cramping the names on the form, which may lead to errors. For additional versions of the individual's name (married, professional, commonly known as or nickname), use the additional blank spaces on the form, or a second sheet, if necessary.

Referring to the table in the upper left corner of the worksheet, start with the vowels and write the numerical value for each on the first blank line, directly beneath. Do this for each part of the name. Fill out the consonant line as well. Fill out the line for all letters, which will be the combination of the numbers for the vowels and the consonants. Now fill in the three lines of numbers for any other versions of the name.

Proceed to add the numbers for each part of each name and write the sum in parentheses at the right end of each section. Do this for the vowels, consonants and all letters. At the extreme right, just in front of the printed numerals one, two, and three, write the sums of the values for all three parts of the name for the vowels, consonants and all letters. Reduce each of these sums to a single digit (add the individual digits together once, twice or more until they are reduced to a single digit (except, don't reduce 11 or 22 any further) and write the values to the right of the three numbers (one, two and three.)

From the following sections, find the meanings of the numerological value of each of the three analyses for each version of the name and write them in abbreviated form in the blank spaces provided, in the Descriptions area. For an example, see the analysis of William Jefferson Clinton following those descriptive sections.

VOWELS—INNER URGE OR MOTIVATION (ALSO CALLED INNER DESIRE, SECRET AMBITIONS, PERSONAL INCLINATIONS AND SOUL LONGING)

A "ONE" *Inner Urge*

Desire to succeed, lead or dominate. Not a detail person, but one who pushes the overall plan or project forward to completion. Could be very impatient. Delights in seeking and receiving praise. Might be boastful and self-seeking. Will likely "go it alone" rather than join in a cooperative effort.

A "TWO" *Inner Urge*

Contrary to the number "ONE," the number "TWO" seeks cooperation with others and is more of a follower than a leader. Is involved in partnership or association with others. Is sensitive, emotional and friendly; seeks companionship and marriage. Is loving and affectionate and likes comfort, but is not especially hardworking.

A "THREE" *Inner Urge*

Like the number "TWO," this person is outgoing and friendly, but has a stronger need for self-expression. Is a lover of beauty in people and surroundings.

A "FOUR" *Inner Urge*

This is a hard worker who is steady and dependable. Loves tradition and order in home and at work. Is not comfortable with spontaneity or change, but desires a regular schedule of activity.

A "FIVE" *Inner Urge*

Is a freedom lover who welcomes and even seeks change. Is very adaptable and has varied interests. Loves to travel and enjoy life.

A "SIX" *Inner Urge*

A family person who accepts responsibility and a life of service. Is very understanding and often in the role of a peacemaker. A good person to turn to with your problems if you desire a sympathetic listener.

A "SEVEN" Inner Urge

Usually a quiet thinker and dreamer who prefers to be by him/herself and may even live alone. Usually intellectual and philosophical, a conservative person who doesn't share thoughts and feelings with others. Enjoys quiet, peaceful surroundings with time to contemplate, meditate and dream. Finds menial tasks a bore and is not very open to change.

An "EIGHT" Inner Urge

An executive type, probably involved in big business or financial activities such as investing. Seeks accumulation of wealth and power with confidence and little apprehension of the outcome.

A "NINE" Inner Urge

A learner and teacher who loves to share knowledge with others. Would rather use his/her knowledge and experience to help others than for his/her own benefit.

An "ELEVEN" Inner Urge

An idealist with a broad outlook. Like the "NINE" person, above, he/she is a learner and loves to share knowledge with others, however the knowledge imparted is about God and spiritual matters. May experience inspiration and revelation and feel compelled to be a messenger of information from higher realms.

A "TWENTY-TWO" Inner Urge

Like the "ELEVEN," this master number imparts an even more universal outlook as far as humanity and spirituality, with even less concern for the self. The individual is usually an intelligent person with high ideals, but living a rather ordinary life as far as position or material status.

CONSONANTS — INNER SELF OR IMPRESSION (ALSO KNOWN AS PASSIVE MOODS AND WHAT YOU'RE LIKE WHEN YOU'RE ALONE)

The vibration of the Inner Self is found by adding the values of all the consonants of the name and reducing the total to a single digit (or to eleven or twenty-two). The Inner Self is the quiet, and usually hidden, part deep within which embodies a desire to accomplish or achieve along certain lines.

Inner Self Numbers: Keywords

"ONE"—Initiative, Leadership
"TWO"—Partnership, Companionship, Association
"THREE"—Creativity, Communication,
   Self-expression
"FOUR"—Productivity, Work
"FIVE"—Adaptability, Change, Freedom
"SIX"—Service, Responsibility, Order
"SEVEN"—Study, Learning, Meditation
"EIGHT"—Executive, Finance, Material Leadership

"NINE"—Completion, Service

"ELEVEN"—Spiritual Learning and Teaching

"TWENTY-TWO"—Humanitarian, Spiritual Builder

ALL LETTERS—OUTER SELF OR EXPRESSION (WHAT YOU EXPRESS TO THE WORLD)

The Outer Self is found from the sum of all the letters in the name. Another way of looking at it is that it's the total of the addition of the Inner Urge and the Inner Self. This is what is expressed to others, outwardly. It is the complete makeup of the individuality, with all its negative, as well as positive, aspects. It's synonymous with personality.

OUTER SELF NUMBERS (ALL LETTERS)

A "ONE" Outer Self: A leader who is not influenced by others. Ambitious and creative. A strong desire to accomplish, achieve and be successful. Beware: Being insensitive to the opinions and needs of others. Don't let the ego run wild.

A "TWO" Outer Self: A team worker who cooperates with others in any endeavor. Usually married. May be in a business partnership. Beware: Depending on others too much for material or emotional needs.

A "THREE" Outer Self: Creative, expressive, friendly, social. Usually involved in some form of the arts such as painting, sculpting, music, writing, drama, fashions or decorating. Beware: Don't overdo the self-expression when with others—let the other person get a word in.

A "FOUR" Outer Self: Hardworking, productive, traditional,

usually employed by others. This person is not very open to new methods and changes of routine. Beware: This person is solid and dependable, but must be careful not to be overly taciturn, stern, or a drag to others by being cut off from the everyday pleasures of life. Don't be a workaholic!

A "FIVE" Outer Self: A lover of freedom and travel. Welcomes change and variety in life. Sociable and knowledgeable. Beware: Lack of responsibility and care, especially with personal relationships. Avoid overindulgence.

A "SIX" Outer Self: A person who accepts responsibility and holds home and family in high regard. This person is well balanced, stable and understanding. Beware: Not giving others some breathing room and giving in to jealousy. Allow others, especially family members, to make their own mistakes.

A "SEVEN" Outer Self: A philosopher, a seeker of truth and the meaning of life. Seeks to learn of the spiritual side of life. Studious, quiet and keeps thoughts private. Beware: Giving the impression of aloofness or insensitivity. Avoid getting into a state of sadness or depression.

An "EIGHT" Outer Self: Big-business executive type on a drive for success and wealth. Self-confident and aggressive. Beware: Ambition for money and power can cause hardness and insensitivity to the wants and needs of others. Personal relationships may suffer.

A "NINE" Outer Self: A person with a broad outlook based on past experiences (not just from this life). One who seeks and teaches truth. Beware: Being impractical or negative about one's restrictions.

An "ELEVEN" Outer Self: A searcher for truth and knowledge, especially in the higher, spiritual areas of life. One who may experience inspiration and revelation. Beware: Fanaticism or considering yourself superior to others.

A "TWENTY-TWO" Outer Self: Idealist, creator and builder on a humanitarian scope. One who pursues his/her vision based on inspiration and faith. Beware: Being involved in projects just for personal gain or self-promotion.

ANALYSIS OF THE NAME

Most numerology experts agree that the original name given at birth is the one to use for determining the numbers that relate to a person. For names that are changed, please refer to the chapter Numerology for Success. For an example of name analysis, we are using William Jefferson Clinton. There is a blank format for name analysis in the appendix, which you may photocopy for your own use.

Full Name:	WILLIAM	JEFFERSON	CLINTON
1. Vowels:	9 9 1 (19)	5 5 6 (16)	9 6 (15) = 50 = 5
2. Consonants:	5 3 3 4 (15)	1 6 6 9 1 5 (28)	3 3 5 2 5 (18) = 61 = 7
3. All Letters:	5 9 3 3 9 1 4 (34)	1 5 6 6 5 9 1 6 5 (44)	3 3 9 5 2 6 5 (33) = 111 = 3

It is not necessary to put down the numbers of all the letters, since simply adding the total values of the vowels and consonants will give the same result. I included all the numbers so that you can add them up and satisfy yourself that it comes out the same either way. Remember that some numerologists feel that a K has the value of eleven and a V has the value of twenty-two when they are found in a name. Try it both ways to see if it makes a difference. It probably will not, but it will be edifying for you to go through the exercise. There are also some rules about whether Y and W are considered consonants or vowels. If a Y is preceded by another vowel or if there is no other vowel in a syllable, then it is handled like a vowel. If a W is combined with another vowel in a single sound, it is considered a vowel.

We see that William Jefferson Clinton breaks down as follows:

Inner Urge or Motivation (vowels): 5
Inner Self or Impression (consonants): 7
Outer Self or Expression (all letters): 3

See the descriptions of these number vibrations in the earlier part of this chapter. Basically, Bill Clinton's motivation indicates one who loves freedom and travel. He is very adaptable, with many interests, and loves to enjoy life. His Inner Urge is that of a serious student who loves learning and may even seek enlightenment or guidance through quiet meditation. The "THREE" outer self is that of a friendly, expressive and creative person who loves the arts and is usually personally involved in some form of art (Hmm, music? . . . The saxophone, I believe).

FULL NUMBER VALUE OR CHARACTERISTIC
OF EACH LETTER OF THE ALPHABET

In some schools of numerology, such as that derived from the Kabbalah, each letter of the alphabet has its own individual vibration, which is represented by its full number value. Following is a modern, widely accepted, full number-characteristic list of the twenty-six letters of the English alphabet. It is to be noted that in some of the cases of individuals listed as examples, professional pen names or stage names are given which differ from their birth names. This, too, is valid because use of a different name over a period of time changes the vibration around a person, often to one more suitable for the activity in which one wishes to engage.

A (1)—Initiative and leadership, creativity and originality, indicates strong will and determination when it's the first letter in a name. If it's the first vowel, it indicates a domineering nature. Examples: Andre Aggasi, in 1999 he was the U.S. Open Champion for the second time, and top-rated player in the world. Also, Alexander the Great, Attila the Hun, Emperor Augustus, Mark Antony, Archimedes, Aristotle, Ethan Allen, Samuel Adams and Allan Alda.

B (2)—Partnership, collaboration, willingness to cooperate. An emotional nature is indicated when it's the first letter of a name. If it's the first consonant after a vowel, it indicates an introspective and analytical nature with a depth of understanding. Examples: Humphrey Bogart, Lauren Bacall, George Burns, Lucille Ball, Sonny Bono, Mel Brooks, Ann Bancroft, General Omar Bradley, and Abraham Lincoln.

C (3)—Creative intellect and self-expression. When the first consonant in a name, it indicates optimism and a healthy emotional nature. Examples: Copernicus, Truman Capote, Frank Capra, John Calvin, John Candy, Al Capp, Billy Crystal, James Cann, Sid Caesar, Erskine Caldwell, Maria Callas, Thomas Carlyle, Andrew Carnegie, Lewis Carroll, Johnny Cash, Charlie Chaplin, Chevy Chase, Cher, Chekov, Chopin and Sir Winston Churchill.

D (4)—As the first letter or appearing a number of times in a name, it can signify restriction and limitation. A person with such a name should strive to rise above any restrictions and become a more developed and admirable individual. Examples: King David, President Dwight David Eisenhower, entertainers Phyllis Diller, Danny DeVito and Rodney Dangerfield (no respect!).

E (5)—Intellectual, mental, this letter signifies communication. E is the most commonly used vowel and letter in the English language. It is like a cornerstone of the language. If it's the first letter or vowel in a name, it indicates an ability to write, lecture, speak publicly, sing or engage in any activity where words are used. If E appears a number of times in the name, there is a strong likelihood that the person will be involved in one or more of these activities on a regular basis and even reach a degree of fame. Examples: nineteenth-century philosopher and writer Ralph Waldo Emerson, inventor Thomas Alva Edison (also see "A"); mathematicians/scientists Euclid, Euler and Albert Einstein; photographers George Eastman and Alfred Eisenstadt; Greek dramatist Euripedes, screenwriter/producer Blade Edwards, movie critic Roger Ebert, painter El Greco and Christian Science founder Mary Baker Eddy.

F (6)—Indicates domestic involvement, care of the home and family, and achievement of a high degree of happiness through home and family. Think of the word "Father." It denotes an adult point of view and indicates a high degree of protection and providing for family members. Material matters are handled well by a person with several Fs in the name. Examples: actors Henry Fonda, Preston Foster and Charles Farrell.

G (7)—Denotes an introspective nature, involved in study and meditation, with the desire to understand oneself and the world. A number of Gs in the name indicates a keen analytical nature, able to determine the truth of peoples' motivations. Psychic perception is a likely attribute. Examples: Mohandas Gandhi, Gautama Buddha and evangelist Billy Graham.

H (8)—Great potential for material success, if handled well. The ossibilities for loss are great also, if errors are made. If H is the first letter of the name, the individual has strong potential for success or failure in material matters. Along with this, of course, is development of character. We've all read stories or seen movies about a character who is blessed with an abundance of material return and then takes advantage of others in his business dealings or his personal life and winds up losing everything. This is based on real life. The people who travel this path in real life probably have an H as the first letter of their names. These people generally have a magnetic personality. They should use it in being fair and kind to others as well as for their own growth and happiness. Examples: Japanese Emperor Hirohito, labor leader James Hoffa, publisher William Randolph Hearst and novelist Ernest Hemingway.

I (9)—If I is the first letter or first vowel of the name, it indicates a spiritual or psychic nature with tolerance and sympathy for others. If repeated in the name it may denote too great a degree of sensitivity and, therefore, sadness. This should be guarded against. As Emerson said, "Your goodness must have an edge to it or it be not goodness at all." Don't let others take advantage of you. They have their own soul agendas in this life and must use their own free will to learn their own lessons and overcome their own life situations. Examples: Saint Ignatius de Loyola and Archbishop Iakovos (recipient of 1980 Presidential Medal of Freedom).

J (10)—Like the A (1), this letter indicates leadership if it's the first consonant in the name or occurs a number of times. Since it's a higher octave of number one*, it indicates a higher sta-

---

*In a general sense, any two-digit number that can be numerologically reduced to a single digit (10: 1+0 = 1) is a higher octave of that digit. For example, the master numbers eleven and twenty-two are higher octaves of two and four.

tion in life and gain or profit from new ideas, concepts or devices. It also denotes a magnetic personality and involvement with cultural or intellectual activities. Examples: President Thomas Jefferson and psychoanalyst Carl Gustav Jung.

K (11)—This letter, which vibrates to a higher octave of two, when in a name, engenders a magnetic personality combining the force of a one and the cooperative nature of two. It promotes strength and endurance. If it's the first consonant in a name, it indicates a love and aptitude for dramatics such as theater and other forms of public entertainment. Examples: President John F. Kennedy, Henry Kissinger and actress Madeline Kahn.

L (12)—If the first consonant of your name or if repeated therein a number of times, it denotes sociability, good character and a degree of success. You would also have a reliable intuition that you should call upon when needed. This helps you to understand the motives of others. Rely on your first impressions for responding to people or situations. This letter also denotes a romantic nature and an active life. Examples: TV show hosts Jay Leno and David Letterman.

M (13)—This letter indicates strength and stability. It denotes an orderly mind with the ability to concentrate and study. When M is the first consonant in a name, it signifies a noble, hardworking nature with a love of a peaceful home life. The individual is a searcher for spiritual enlightenment. If it appears a number of times in the name, it indicates strong determination and a never-say-die nature. Examples: actress Shirley MacLaine, Israeli Prime Minister Golda Meir, author Margaret Mitchell and artist Michelangelo.

N (14)—This letter has a receptive quality on a nonphysical level whereby the individual will be able to tune in to new concepts, ideas and music, seemingly out of nowhere. It denotes an alert nature that seems to have the ability to perceive and attract that which is an advantage to itself. If it's the first letter or consonant in a name, it imparts the ability of flexibility but may lead to scattering of talents and efforts. Examples: prophet Nostradamus and mathematician/scientist Sir Isaac Newton.

O (15)—The shape of this letter symbolizes the universe. It signifies responsibility on the material level. In the name, O endows balance, intellectual capacity and a very capable nature. The person with this letter prominent in his or her name will be very centered in home, family and business, with love and affection in large measure. Such a person may find that life is rather circumscribed within narrow limits, but will enjoy a great degree of spiritual growth. Examples: international shipping magnate Aristotle Onassis and poet Omar Khayyam.

P (16)—If the first letter or consonant of the name, it indicates mental clarity and foresight. A number of Ps in the name can engender success and power. However, caution is needed to hold what is gained. Precaution should be exercised in all endeavors, since this vibration can lead in a negative direction as well as along positive lines. Guidance should be sought through meditation and study of spiritual philosophy. Examples: Pope Pius XII and Padre Pia.

Q (17)—This vibration is of a dual nature, incorporating both physical force and mysticism. It engenders success both in spiritual and material matters. With Q in the name in any position, great material success can be achieved. It also endows a magnetic quality to the individual. Examples: Aztec god Quetzalcoatl and actor Anthony Quinn.

R (18)—This letter in the name endows great power. When R is the first letter or consonant of the name, the bearer must exercise discrimination in using his or her potential for positive rather than negative purposes. Much good can be achieved by the proper use of this energy. Examples: Theodore Roosevelt, Ronald Reagan, Rosanne Barr.

S (19)—This letter symbolizes the start of a new cycle. The number nineteen contains the two extremes of the basic nine digits. Likewise S indicates the striving of man toward spiritual mastery. In a name it engenders a strong creative impulse along nonmaterial lines. Examples: William Shakespeare, Socrates, and religious leader Joseph Smith.

T (20)—This letter, which resembles the cross, symbolizes ultimate sacrifice for the benefit of mankind. When it is the first letter or consonant in a name, it denotes a cooperative nature that will follow and build upon what others have started. It indicates flexibility and devotion. Examples: novelist Leo Tolstoi, Mother Teresa (Nobel Peace Prize winner) and Terence Cardinal Cooke.

U (21)—Like an open cup, this letter can gather material and personal blessings, but must be carefully balanced to avoid spilling out the contents. If U is the first vowel or appears a number of times in your name, it promises the receipt of many blessings in life. It endows popularity, success and pleasure, but care must be taken to maintain a sense of balance and fairness so that what is gained will not be scattered and dissipated. Examples: actress Tracey Ullman, football star Johnny Unitas and auto racer Al Unser.

V (22)—Like eleven, twenty-two is a master number. The letter V in a name engenders the desire and ability to study advanced metaphysics. It involves hard work followed by gratifying rewards. Spiritual knowledge is put into practice on this material plane. V is called the letter of demonstration, whereby celestial visions are brought into visible forms. Examples: philosopher/writer Voltaire, composer Guiseppe Verdi, author Jules Verne and the Roman poet Virgil.

W (23)—This letter denotes change from old conditions to new. This can be a shock to the person undergoing the change. The person with a W in his or her name must learn to be flexible and accept change. If this letter appears two or more times in the name, it indicates a love of excitement, speed, travel and the dramatic. Example: Orson Welles.

X (24)—This letter rarely occurs in English-language names. Its influence is very self-effacing. It indicates a very high degree of spiritual love, humanitarianism, and responsibility. The bearer of a name with this letter prominent is likely to put his or her ego aside and work to alleviate the suffering of humanity. Example: Saint Francis Xavier.

Y (25)—With this letter in the name, the individual is a seeker and searcher of the greater mysteries of life. This letter, similar in shape to a divining rod, indicates a person who craves knowledge of the esoteric, of what lies behind physical, material life. It may be a life of spiritual study and meditation, as well as one of humane service, which leads to great rewards of understanding and wisdom on the higher levels. Example: Mormon founder Brigham Young.

Z (26)—Like the eight and other higher octaves of eight,* this letter has enormous potential for power and material gain, but it can lead in a positive or negative path, depending on the individual. Restraint and discrimination must be employed, along with a high spiritual purpose, to avoid self-destruction and to enjoy the great rewards that this energy offers. Examples: writer Emile Zola, theatrical producer Florenz Ziegfeld, movie producer Daryl Zanuck and singer/songwriter Frank Zappa.

---

*A higher octave of a number is simply a two-digit value whose individual digits add up to that number. For example, 8: 17 (1+7 = 8), 26 (2+6 = 8) 35 (3+5 = 8) and 44 (4+4 = 8).

NAME NUMEROLOGY WORKSHEET NO. I

At this point, if you have not already done so, we suggest that you turn to Appendix 2 at the end of the book and make copies of the three worksheets. If possible, use a copier with an enlarging feature to make full-size masters (the maximum size that will fit on an 8½-by-11 sheet of paper). You can then use these masters on any copier to make any number of worksheet forms to use when analyzing names. At this time it's suggested that you fill in Worksheet No. 1 with the birth name and other forms of the name that you wish to analyze. If there are more than three forms of the person's name, use a second page of Worksheet No. 1. The first form should be the name the person was given at the time of birth, and which is on the birth certificate. The second form should be the name with which the person was christened if it is different from that on the birth certificate. The next form should be that which the person most commonly uses and is known by in everyday life. For instance, many people don't use their middle name very often. Their associates, friends and even some family members may not know their middle name. Other forms of the person's name may include a commonly used nickname, a stage name or writer's nom de plume.

The given name at birth is always the most significant, especially in the early, formative years of life, and must always be considered in any evaluation. If the christened name is different, then we feel the two should be given equal weight. The name form that is commonly used grows more significant through the years, especially with friends and business associates or coworkers. Of course, a name used in connection with a career such as acting or writing, and by which one becomes known to large numbers of people, is especially significant in that career. Analyze all forms of the name and write out the resultant descriptions. Apply the descriptions with discrimination to the applicable areas of life. We expect you will see that the character, personality, motivation, likes and dislikes of a person will have gone through changes that relate to the changing forms of the name used through the years.

Neatly print the name or forms of the name in the spaces provided. If there are more than three names in the full name, use a second page of the worksheet, listing the full name across the two sheets, rather than trying to cram it all onto one sheet, which may cause errors. Carefully determine the numerological value of each letter for the vowels, for the consonants and for all letters in the name (combine the vowels and the consonants). Add the values for each part of the name (first, middle and last) and list the sum at the right of each section. Add these values and write the sum at the far right. Reduce each of these values to a single digit and write it in the appropriate space at the extreme right for 1 (vowels), 2 (consonants) or 3 (all letters). Refer to the three lists of descriptions; Inner Urge or Motivation (vowels), Inner Self or Impression (consonants) and Outer Self (all letters), near the beginning of this chapter. Write the particular description for each on one of the three lines under the heading: Descriptions.

Next, examine the name for significant letters; that is, letters at the beginning of a name or those that appear a number of times in the name. Note that the letter E is so common in the English language that it is not considered significant unless it appears more than twice or as a first letter plus at least one other place. List the significant letters (there may be several) one below the other in the designated areas of the worksheet. Look up the characteristics of these letters in the list starting on page 140 of this chapter and write them next to each significant letter. This will pretty well fill the available space on Worksheet No. 1.

Proceed to Worksheet No. 2 for further name analysis. On this worksheet, print the version of the name with which you are working and write in the three values (vowels, consonants and all letters) you determined from the first worksheet. The first analysis of this worksheet is the three challenges. For the first challenge, find the value of the first vowel and that for the last vowel of the name. Subtract the lesser value from the larger and put down the result in the space provided. For the second challenge, find the values of the first and last consonants of the name. Subtract the lesser value from the greater and put the result in the space provided on the second line. For the third challenge, simply add the first and second values and place this sum in the space on the third line. For the descriptions of the challenges, see Appendix 3. These name challenges indicate the lessons that we are to learn in this lifetime.

INCLUSION

The inclusion of the name is simply how many times each number, from one through nine, comes up in the name. Some numerals (based on the letters in the name) may occur a number of times, some, not at all. From the analysis of the name on Worksheet No. 1, using the full name and all letters (vowels and consonants) fill in the little chart that looks like a tic-tac-toe game on Worksheet No. 2. Notice the arrangement of the nine numerals in this chart and fill in the number of times each occurs in the name in the corresponding space in the blank chart. Where there is no occurrence, write "0." From the Inclusion section of Appendix 4, read the indications listed for each number, depending on whether there is a normal number of occurrences (one or two), an overabundance (three or more) or a lack due to no occur-

rences. Note: Due to the E being so common in the English language, divide the number of occurrences of five due to Es by two.
This will put matters into a more proper proportion. The inclu-
sions represent abilities or development we have brought over
from past lives. In some cases we may be overdeveloped; in others
we may have a lack that we should be working on in this lifetime.

HIDDEN PASSION

This is a strong inner drive that motivates us along certain lines.
It is shown by the number that occurs most often in the name. In
some cases there may be two or even three numbers that occur
very frequently (three or more times). Be sure to divide the number of Es by two. See the interpretations of these frequently appearing numbers in Appendix 5.

CHALLENGES

Challenges to the Hidden Passion are where there were no occurrences in the name of certain numbers. These indicate weaknesses in our development. Refer to the meanings in Appendix 5
and consider these areas as where we should expend extra time
and effort to round out our individual development.

SUBCONSCIOUS SELF

The consensus of numerologists is that this analysis signals our
reaction when confronted with a problem or emergency. It is said
to also apply when we come across a new concept, idea or task. It

is not premeditated or planned, but more of a reflex action. It is determined by subtracting the number of zeros (no occurrence of certain numbers) in the name from nine. For example, if there were three numbers that didn't occur in the name, then subtract three from nine, leaving six. Six would be the indicator of the subconscious reaction. Look up the meanings in Appendix 5. Note that four is the lowest number that occurs in this process. We personally don't think much of this particular name analysis. It is too negative. It is unfairly harsh for short names with no middle name. For example, the name Jay Fox has only three number values (one for J and A, seven for Y and six for F, O and X). With six missing values, the resultant Subconscious Self number is only three, which is not even listed by most numerologists. However, there it is, a fairly common short English name (not everybody has a middle name) that has only three numbers. Why it is necessary to go through the subtraction of the quantity of missing numbers from nine in the first place, I don't know. It is simply the number of numerological values that are in the name. Let's keep it simple. English versions of some foreign names also have very few number values in them. We do not perceive how this lack of number values in the name relates to Karmic lessons, but we are including this analysis in its usual form for completeness.

CORNERSTONE

The cornerstone is the numerical value of the first letter of the first name. It denotes the foundation of the person's life. It represents the basic characteristic of our inner being. It should be compared to the Expression to see if it increases or modifies it. Refer to the list of the basic meanings of the numbers found in Chapter 2.

FIRST VOWEL

The first vowel of a name signifies an important character trait of the Inner Self. It is the temperament or disposition, how we could be counted on to behave in a given situation. See the list of first-vowel characteristics in Appendix 5.

KEY

The key portends how the life will be lived. It is the numerological value of the first name (the sum of the individual letter values, reduced to a single digit). Refer to the list of the basic meanings of numbers found in Chapter 2.

KEY LETTER

This is the numerical value of the initial letter of the last name (surname). This indicates what goal in life will be pursued. Refer to the list of the basic meanings of numbers found in Chapter 2.

ECCENTRICITY

The eccentricity represents the manner in which we would respond to a distressing situation that cropped up in our everyday life. This is found by adding the Key to the day of birth and reducing to a single digit. Refer to the list in Appendix 5.

BALANCE NUMBER

The balance number is the balance of the character, what the individual can fall back on in trying circumstances. It is found by taking the three initials of the full name, adding the letter number values together and reducing to a single digit. Use the list of the basic meanings of numbers found in Chapter 2.

CAPSTONE

The Capstone marks the manner that we react to daily life situations. It is represented by the last letter in the first name. Using the numerical value of that letter, refer to the basic list of meanings in Chapter 2. Also see the complete list of each letter of the alphabet in Chapter 7.

KEYSTONE

The Keystone is an additional personality characteristic and is found to be the middle letter of the first name, therefore it does not exist in first names with an even number of letters. Refer to the full alphabet list in Appendix 5.

NAME CHARACTERISTIC

The name characteristic is found from the total number of letters in the full name. It adds insight to the character and nature of the life of the individual. We would not, personally, put too much stock in this analysis, since some descriptions can be a bit negative or even frightening. Use any undesirable descriptions as a warning to keep in the back of your mind and to guard against. See Appendix 6 for a list of characteristics related to the reduced values of 1 through 9, 11 and 22. There is also a long list running from ten letters through forty-four letters for descriptions based on the actual full (unreduced) number of letters in the name.

REALITY NUMBER

The Reality Number, also known as the Life Number, is extremely important. It is a prime motivator that operates throughout our lives and can show us our life purpose. It can show us why we've made certain choices in our life and guide us to greater success. It is determined by adding the Life Path Number (full birth date) to the Expression (the full name number, using values of all the letters). Refer to Appendix 6 for the list of interpretations of the Reality Number.

PLANES OF EXPRESSION

In astrology the twelve signs are grouped into two sets of categories. There are the four elements of fire, earth, air and water. There are also the three characteristics of cardinal, fixed and mutable. In numerology, the twenty-six letters of the English alphabet fall into two groups of categories, called the Planes of Expression. Similar to the four elements, above, are the categories termed Emotional, Physical, Mental and Intuitive. Similar to the three astrological characteristics, above, are these for the alphabet: Creative, Grounded and Vacillating. The above order of listing these characteristics and the way they're arranged in the table, below, may be different than those of other numerologists. We prefer to put them in the same order as their corresponding astrological characteristics. There is no balanced arrangement of the twenty-six letters in these categories. Some categories have as many as four letters; one category has no letters. The following table shows the twenty-six letters in their appropriate categories. Appendix 2 contains Worksheet No. 4 with this table and a blank one below it. This worksheet may be copied and used for each name to be analyzed for the Planes of Expression.

GUIDE FOR PLACEMENT OF LETTERS IN THE
PLANES OF EXPRESSION

	EMOTIONAL	PHYSICAL	MENTAL	INTUITIVE	TOTALS
Creative	I O R Z	E	A	K	7
Grounded	—	D M	G L	C V	6
Vacillating	B S T X	W	H J N P	F Q U Y	13
Totals	8	4	7	7	26

As can be seen, the unequal number of letters in the various categories yields very different totals. However, notice that four of the five vowels are in the creative category, so we would expect that this would be the most heavily loaded for most English names. This is especially so because E is the most common letter in the English language. Therefore, as in other analyses in this book, we recommend that the number of Es be divided by two.

In the blank form, on page 180, place all the letters of the name in their proper places as many times as they appear in the name. Add up the quantities of the letters in each column and in each row and write them at the bottom and side. As said before, divide the number of Es by two before totaling the various quantities. The greater the quantity in each of the seven characteristics, the greater the strength or influence of that characteristic in the individual. See page 181 and page 182 for descriptions of these seven characteristics.

Chapter 8

Numerology for Success

"Happiness seems to require a modicum of external prosperity."

—*Aristotle*

AN AFFIRMATION THAT
INCREASES PROSPERITY

The following is a perfect affirmation to increase success. It should be memorized and repeated throughout the day to increase the flow of prosperity:

The joy of abundance
Pure milk and honey
My coffer soon
Will be filled with money!

DON'T CURSE THE DARKNESS OR POVERTY — DO SOMETHING!

Throughout the ages many people have recognized and used the power of candles. For instance, burn a green candle along with a white candle for a period of seven days. It will almost always increase prosperity. I suggest that for safety reasons you place both candles in a small bowl of water. I also suggest that you find the seven-day candles that come in a tall glass jar. These candles burn day and night, and are very effective.

LET THE LAW OF FLOW WORK FOR YOU!

"Cast thy bread upon the waters; for thou shalt find it after many days."

—*Old Testament, Ecclesiastes 11:1*

It's also a very good idea to kick the flow of prosperity in your direction by making a charitable contribution to whatever you feel is a worthwhile organization. Let it come from the heart, with as much of a feeling of love as possible.

NUMEROLOGY FOR SUCCESS

"The race is not to the swiftest, nor the battle to the strong."

—*Old Testament, Ecclesiastes 9:2*

For the first step toward the use of numerology for success, we can determine the type of work or business for which we are best suited:

THE NUMBER ONE PERSON—BORN ON THE 1ST, 10TH, 19TH OR 28TH   You are a number one person if you were born on the 1st, 10th, 19th or 28th. Your greatest success comes with positions that involve decision making, authority and everything involved with administration.

Number one people are most fulfilled when there is an emotional involvement in their career. You are happiest when you are able to use your excellent creative potential and organizational abilities. Your natural flair for drama is an important part of your expression. The theater and stage beckon to you, but you can be just as comfortable in vocations involved with luxury and glamour.

Many number one personalities shine as lawyers and judges, and are extremely comfortable in a courtroom setting.

Most number ones are naturally ambitious, and are interested in money chiefly for the luxury or comfort that it can bring. Number ones love shopping and buying beautiful things, especially quality jewelry and clothing. Travel is also high on the number one's list of loves, especially if it is first class!

Number ones are rarely shrinking violets, and love to be seen, heard and appreciated. Number ones love to be in positions of authority, such as employers or bosses, so that they can express as much power and control as possible!

Number ones have an inbred dislike of anything second-rate, shoddy or second-class. This is not someone who will be impressed with your economical or money-saving moves! Number ones will be far more impressed with touches of luxury, class or elegance that have been added to the work front. No penny-pinching allowed with number ones! It's just considered déclassé or inferior.

THE NUMBER TWO PERSON—BORN ON THE 2ND, 11TH, 20TH OR 29TH   You are a number two person if you were born on the 2nd, 11th, 20th or 29th. You are an emotional person who will find emotional success in expressive work such as actor, artist, bank teller, collector, chef, cook, computer expert, dancer, diplomat, editor, domestic engineer, metaphysical or yoga instructor, musician, psychiatrist, poet, author, secretary, statistician or teacher.

The great tenacity and determination of most number two people manifests in many ways. Number twos love variety and changes of scene, changes of heart and change in general. This doesn't necessarily flow over into their career life, however. Number two personalities are able to reflect and remember experiences that occurred earlier in their lives. The beauty of this is that the prior lessons help them to be heads and shoulders above the crowd in current career situations. Number twos express great shrewdness, and manifest an extraordinary amount of instinct and intuition.

The number two personality more than corners the market when it comes to caring and compassion. Number twos, therefore, often find themselves in the capacity of caretakers, and serve well in hospitals and institutions. The number two's imagination is also superior to other people's. Therefore they often find themselves in a capacity involving working for movies or in the theater. Number twos also excel in working on anything from the past; for instance, careers involved with antiques, antiquing, and museum work.

Number two-type people have a finely tuned sense of aesthetics, and love to express that talent with food! Number two people are usually the best chefs.

Number twos can often make a great deal of money in their lifetimes. However, they occasionally suffer from the condition of fear, that causes them to be what's often known as tight-fisted, or economical.

Number twos are excellent teachers, professors, lecturers, or teachers of young children.

Number twos are eager to make money, and like to hoard it whenever possible.

THE NUMBER THREE PERSON—BORN ON THE 3RD, 12TH, 21ST OR 30TH   The number three person is born on the 3rd, 12th, 21st or 30th. You most likely will find creative expression and success in work such as acting, art, administration, entertainment, fashion design, law, jewelry, government, politics, religion, photography, publishing, sales, social work or writing.

Number three people usually have careers that involve caring or compassion. Number threes have moderately good organizational skills, and can work selflessly behind the scenes. They are also good, however, with any careers that involve the use of their creative or imaginary talents, such as acting and writing. Number threes can be quite self-effacing, and are capable of hiding or undermining their personalities.

Their compassionate natures help them to work with those who are suffering or in some kind of distress or need. However, they are also strongly attracted to all trades and expression involved with glamour, art and the theater. Many number threes are also attracted to religious orders, or jobs that will allow them to be helpful to others.

Many number threes will have two jobs at one time. One

position will be lucrative, and the other less so, but possibly more satisfying. The number three personality is flexible, and most likely enjoys a variety of expressions. Strict, tight routines may be quite challenging to a number three type of personality.

THE NUMBER FOUR PERSON—BORN ON THE 4TH, 13TH, 22ND OR 31ST   You are a number four person if you were born on the 4th, 13th, 22nd or 31st. You will most likely find your greatest success in jobs such as being an accountant, pilot, electrician, engineer, inventor, investigator, manufacturer, mathematician, mechanic, motorman, musician, optometrist, TV or radio personality, radiologist, printer, reformer or sculptor.

Number four personalities love a challenge. Boring, repetitive work should be avoided. You must have free rein to do whatever is expected of you, in your own way, and in your own time! Continual advice or the insistence on a particular type of pattern or regime cannot inhibit you. You have to express your inventiveness in your work, whether creative, scientific or (Heaven forbid) pragmatic. You will always have a unique approach to any problem or situation. Many number fours become inventors. Others succeed in communications, or possibly the technical areas of television, radio and the Internet. Airline careers are often a number four pursuit. There will also be a strong sense of caring about their fellow human beings, and an involvement in humanitarian work.

Many number fours are also found in social work and administration for large charitable organizations. Not usually obsessive about income, number fours should remember that "charity begins at home."

THE NUMBER FIVE PERSON—BORN ON THE 5TH, 14TH OR 23RD   The number five person, born on the 5th,

14th or 23rd, will most often find work as an astrologer, real-estate broker or mogul, detective, writer or editor, importer/exporter, medical technician or lab worker, musician, pilot, public official, promoter, racing car driver, mathematician, salesman, scientist, entrepreneur, travel agent, wholesaler or author.

The number five person usually excels at communication skills, as well as all media and Internet work. Many number fives can be found in accounting, commercial travel and public relations.

In business, number fives are usually the most cunning and crafty of employees. Number fives usually do their best work privately, and then publicly dazzle everyone! Most number five people epitomize the "swimming swan theory of success. . . ." That is, they paddle fast and furiously beneath the surface of the water. No one realizes from their calm, collected demeanor and presentation the amount of effort and work that goes on beneath the surface.

Number fives have to be aware that they can be their own worst enemy. Number fives can have such quick mental energy that they may appear superficial, and can occasionally lack the persistence needed to finish jobs or assignments.

THE NUMBER SIX PERSON—BORN ON THE 6TH, 15TH OR 24TH   The number six person, born on the 6th, 15th or 24th, will find harmony and success in work such as therapist, psychiatrist, artist, beautician or hair stylist, cashier, civil servant, counselor, fashion designer, healer, doctor, dentist, attorney, musician, nurse, professor, social worker, surgeon, teacher or waiter.

The number six person is hardworking and ambitious, and enjoys setting up a solid career pattern for future success. When it comes to income, there has to be an element of steadiness and reliability. Risk is not something that most number six people relish. Just about anything unpredictable is not high on the list of favorite things for this person. While financial security is important to number six people, so are inner peace, harmony and aesthetics.

Material security and success are primary interests. Number six people often find themselves, therefore, in careers where they may have "sold out" simply because of the material rewards. Number sixes are practical people who are very good at careers connected with money, such as banking, insurance and the stock exchange. While sixes don't take kindly to risk, the rewards may help them to overcome their trepidation.

Number sixes succeed at taking a "seed" idea from scratch, and seeing it all the way to the end. In most cases, that means prosperity.

THE NUMBER SEVEN PERSON—BORN ON THE 7TH, 16TH OR 25TH   The number seven person is born on the 7th, 16th or 25th. Number seven people will find success in work such as healer, astrologer, psychic, astronomer, metaphysician, secret agent, scientist, computer specialist, technician, medical assistant, medical doctor, researcher, physical therapist, chiropractor, X-ray technician, filmmaker, boat builder or sailor.

The key to success for number sevens lies in the ability for their work to encompass the seen as well as the unseen. That relates to the physical as well as nonphysical worlds. There also has to be an involvement with the number seven's emotions and feelings. Number sevens are willing to work hard, but only if their body, mind and soul are involved. Financial security is important, and number sevens are willing to work hard for all that they achieve.

However, in all their efforts, there may always be an overtone of sensitivity, possibly moodiness and emotional reaction. What sevens bring to the table, though, is the ability to intuitively understand problems, and to troubleshoot with great perception. Number sevens are, however, willing to work hard to achieve and maintain financial stability and, in some cases, a great living. It is very important for sevens to stay challenged, or unreasonable despair and discouragement can be a factor.

THE NUMBER EIGHT PERSON—BORN ON THE 8TH, 17TH OR 26TH   The number eight person, who is born on the 8th, 17th or 26th, often finds the greatest success in a position of decision-making authority: banking, contracting, building, criminal expert, religious official, composer, controller, corporate lawyer, financial expert, accountant, government official, farmworker, miner, mathematician, political organizer, police officer, public or political figure, philosopher, repairperson or personnel interviewer.

The number eight person thrives on responsibility and power. The number eights love getting the job done, and done properly . . . even if it does take a big longer to do it right. Number eight people are usually incredibly thorough, with great attention to those annoying little details. While keeping all of this in mind, they never stop attempting to climb the ladder of success. Even when that's accomplished, they don't stop. They will continue to find bigger and better goals.

With all of this hard work going on, the number eight person rarely displays a reckless attitude toward money. There is a definite respect and fondness for cash!

THE NUMBER NINE PERSON—BORN ON THE 9TH, 18TH, OR 27TH   Number nine people are born on the 9th, 18th or 27th. Number nines find their greatest success in work such as being an artist, athlete, hair stylist, military expert, firefighter, militia expert, political activist, attorney, community or national leader or spokesperson, iron worker, metal worker, politician, newspaper or magazine publisher, steel worker or surgeon.

The number nine person is so freedom loving! In addition, their independent, strongly opinionated, sure-footed attitude and capabilities all add up to success. Number nine people usually achieve all or most of what they attempt to achieve. They are not quitters! If you need something done, and done well, ask a number nine person. It may not be exactly what you had in mind, but it will most likely be done admirably.

The number nine person works best under pressure, and with deadlines, as long as the carrot of success or achievement is in view. This person can be impatient, which isn't necessarily a bad thing. Sometimes, you just have to know when to quit, and to stop wasting your time, or better yet, stop throwing good money after bad. Number nine people usually have an impeccable sense of timing, and instinctively know when to call it a day.

Number nines have entrepreneurial ability, and incredible discernment in dealing with people. All great keys to success.

SEED THOUGHTS FOR SECRETS OF SUCCESS

If you were born on the 1st—Believe in, and express the truth, rather than opinion—even if you are the source of that opinion!

If you were born on the 2nd—Have faith in your own work; see it as a service to mankind, and not just as a means of personal gain.

If you were born on the 3rd—Fine-tune your ability to meditate and focus on whatever task you set for yourself.

If you were born on the 4th—Welcome and embrace growth opportunities, whatever hurdles confront you.

If you were born on the 5th—View each day as a new beginning, bright with promise and hope. Never define yourself as who
and what your past accomplishments were.

If you were born on the 6th—Don't limit your sense of who
you are to what your present situation is—expand that definition
to include your highest potentials.

If you were born on the 7th—Ask yourself in everything you
do, "What would I feel the greatest joy about in doing something
for somebody else?"

If you were born on the 8th—Keep your ears, heart and eyes
open to the truth . . . no matter what the source of that truth may
be.

If you were born on the 9th—Be thankful for your blessings,
no matter how few; do not resent life for what you have not yet
received.

If you were born on the 10th—Stay centered as you meet your
challenges; seek strength, truth and guidance through your own
God-centered reality.

If you were born on the 11th—Fine-tune your human psyche
to the greater will of the Divine.

If you were born on the 12th—Keep your humility strong; remember that pride is the death knell for wisdom and every higher
purpose.

If you were born on the 13th—Remember to do something
not just because it is a popular cause, but because you believe in
your heart center that it is important.

If you were born on the 14th—Make the best of what you
have to work with, rather than wishing about how you think
things should be.

If you were born on the 15th—Without a spark of electricity,
or excitement, nothing worthwhile can be accomplished.

If you were born on the 16th—Rather than asking about

"what's going on here?" try to contribute positive, uplifting energy toward the highest good possible.

If you were born on the 17th—Avoid pointing fingers, or accusing, when things go awry . . . do what you can to turn things around.

If you were born on the 18th—Be as clear as possible about your goals; have the courage and pride to forge ahead with your beliefs.

If you were born on the 19th—See every frustration and thwarted effort as putting you a step closer to greater perfection of spirit.

If you were born on the 20th—Let your goals propel you toward the highest and most lofty expression of your soul.

If you were born on the 21st—Do not allow yourself to be limited to the boundaries of conventional and limited thinking.

If you were born on the 22nd—Never cease to be willing to reevaluate or reconsider your original purposes, ideas or principles.

If you were born on the 23rd—Always tune in to your highest thoughts and innermost feelings before any action . . . make sure your heart always agrees.

If you were born on the 24th—Express the desires of your heart in a state of calm rationale, rather than emotional reaction.

If you were born on the 25th—Take your failures in stride, knowing that you improve with each passing day, and knowing that only God is perfect.

If you were born on the 26th—Know that you are the last word about all of your successes and accomplishments. Great work reflects the genius of its creator.

If you were born on the 27th—Revel in, rather than grumble about, whatever is required for your feeling of accomplishment.

If you were born on the 28th—If you do your very best, and

your efforts are heart-centered, the results will speak for themselves.

If you were born on the 29th—Never cease to set higher and more difficult goals for yourself, never stopping until each goal has been accomplished.

If you were born on the 30th—Guarantee that the results of all of your efforts will be satisfactory by always acting with a positive, generous heart.

If you were born on the 31st—Work toward the best possible, most positive solution, rather than dwelling on the negative problems that present themselves.

A VISUALIZATION TECHNIQUE
TO HELP YOU ACHIEVE SUCCESS

Don't be discouraged if this visualization technique does not work immediately—sometimes a little time has to pass between the time that you express in very clear, concise terms exactly what your heart desires and its realization. The more clearly you can visualize your desires, the more quickly they can manifest. As you visualize your desires, try to see with as much vivid detail as possible all that you hope to accomplish.

Begin by creating a very clear picture of yourself achieving a goal that is important to you. Fill in even more details as you progress in your visualization. Be sure to see yourself clearly in it, or your subconscious will not necessarily know that this goal is for you. If you have difficulties seeing the precise details, such as colors and so forth, then try to feel or sense them.

As you picture the goal in your mind, see yourself achieving this goal. See yourself surrounded by a glowing, golden ball of light. See the ball of light become clearer, brighter and more precise. . . . See the whole imagery of your goal illuminated . . . see it as clearly as possible. Fill in with color wherever you can. . . . See the images take on animated form, coming to life and practically jumping out of your mind's eye.

See the whole picture in front of you glowing and shining brightly, directly in front of you. Again, see as many details as possible. Who's in the picture? What is the time period? Is it now, or does it look like another period of time? How are the people dressed? The more energy you feed into this visualization, the more success you will have with this technique.

See your goal again, surrounded with light, and clearly visible. Mentally, and visually, bring it as close to you as possible. Ask your higher self if there is anything that is keeping your goal from being realized. Perhaps you will intuitively receive an answer that says that "you're not quite ready," or "the time isn't quite right, just now," or a variety of other responses.

Visualize a clear sky, clear setting and perfect visibility. You don't want anything impeding the messages and impressions you will be receiving! See droplets of gold as raindrops coming down from heaven, to increase your prosperity. Know that your power and ability to manifest your heart's desires is becoming increasingly stronger.

Success Secrets for All Birth Dates

1. Be confident! Always say, "Yes, I can do it!" and then go and learn how to do it. You may amaze yourself.
2. Give your word of personal assurance—people will be inclined to trust you, and to listen to what you have to say.
3. Offer positive, proven, tried and true solutions to problems. Usually no one wants to be the first to make a mistake.
4. Say that what you're offering or suggesting will be "effortless"

or "easy" to accomplish. You should have everyone's full attention.

5. Offer the listener something worthwhile, lasting and unusual.

6. Speak briefly about longevity and perfect health and well-being. Make sure your suggestion is very brief, and to the point. Just long enough to get a person's attention.

7. Express the need for "immediate attention" or express the "urgency" of your message. Most people will be concerned, and will listen.

8. Mention the person's name as often as possible. It's the sweetest sound to everyone. Get it right the first time you hear it, write it down if you have to and use it often.

9. Tell your listener that you will be able to save them time and money!

10. Tell the listener that you can offer them something "today," since most people don't have the time or patience to wait for solutions.

11. Tell the listener that you can offer them a very helpful way of making or saving money. Who wouldn't want to do that? Just make sure you have the information to back up your offer.

12. Be emotional! Tell your listener why they will be happier and more fulfilled.

13. Offer an unusual or inventive way to solve a problem, or reinvent an old solution so that it can bring about "satisfactory" or "extremely helpful" results.

14. Recognize and offer an unusual "window of opportunity" when it presents itself. Sometimes it helps to indicate that the opportunity is only for a limited time.

15. Get a person's attention by offering an opportunity for them to be a champion or a winner. Everyone loves to win!

16. Always have as much eye contact as possible with the person you are addressing.

17. Smile, smile, smile!

18. Always try to bring a smile to a person's face, or better yet, make them laugh! Everyone, and I do mean everyone, loves Soupy Sales. I'm proud to say that he's a friend of mine. To my knowledge, he has absolutely no enemies! Even when he is busy, under pressure or rushing, he will always take a moment of his time to tell you a joke!

Make 'em laugh!

APPENDIX 1
CHINESE NUMEROLOGY

"Health is not a condition of matter, but of mind; nor can the material senses bear reliable testimony on the subject of health."

—*Mary Baker Eddy,*
Science and Health

Chinese numerology is a four-thousand-year-old divination tool that started with the Emperor Wu of Hsia. Much of what Emperor Wu discovered about numerology was based on his psychic impressions.

As legend has it, about 2000 BC, Emperor Wu found a tortoise shell on a bank of the Hwang Ho River. What was extraordinary about this tortoise shell were strange markings on it. The markings formed a square, divided into nine smaller squares (three by three), each of which contained one of the nine basic numbers, as follows:

4	9	2
3	5	7
8	1	6

This square is known as the Lo Shu grid and has the curious characteristic that the addition of the three numerals in any row or column, and even diagonally, will total fifteen. It is believed that this "magic square" along with the psychic perception and inspiration of Emperor Wu formed the basics of I Ching, Feng Shui, Chinese astrology and Chinese numerology.

ZHI NENG, A FORM OF CHINESE HEALING THAT USES NUMBERS

Zhi Neng [pronounced ju nung] medicine is one of the newest, most exciting forms of healing. It is based on a powerful method of medical treatment that has been used in China for centuries. Zhi Neng is translated to mean "the amazing capability, capacity and intelligence of the human mind."

Developed by the scholar Guo Zhi Chen, Zhi Neng combines elements of Yin Yang, the Five Elements, the I Ching, Qi Gong, Buddhism and Confucianism, in harmony with Western medicine and scientific beliefs, including biology and physics.

The key to Zhi Neng medicine is that it focuses on the understanding of the link between the vibratory rate of individual cells and a state of wellness or health.

Western medicine pays little or no attention to cellular vibration, which is the primary principle of Zhi Neng. Zhi Neng teaches that too much or too little energy in various areas of the body leads to illness. It also teaches that energy can become blocked in the body, and set it up for infections and poor health. The blocked excess energy causes imbalances, and decreased functioning of various organs. The results may be fatigue, lowered immunity, degenerative changes, swelling or edema, and general malaise.

THE USE OF NUMBERS
IN ZHI NENG HEALING

Zhi Neng healing involves numbers, hand positions, sounds and visualization. For example:

1. The sound *yee-joo*, *yee-joo*, which are the numbers one and nine in Mandarin.

   This sound is used in combination with visualization of light streams coming into the top of the head and flowing throughout the body. This technique is especially effective for lowering or stabilizing blood pressure.

2. The sound *shee yee-joo*, *shee yee-joo*, which are the numbers eleven and nine in Mandarin. The same meditative technique is used for problems related to the eyes.

3. Repeat the sound *san san*, *san san*, the number three in Mandarin, for bronchitis.

4. Repeat the sound *san woo*, *san woo*, the numbers three and five in Mandarin, for colds, and fevers.

5. Repeat the sound *yee woo joo*, *yee woo joo*, the numbers one, five and nine in Mandarin, for dental problems.

6. Repeat the sound *yee yee*, *yee yee*, the number one in Mandarin, for throat problems.

7. Repeat the sound *yee joo*, *yee joo*, the numbers one and nine in Mandarin, for ear inflammation.

8. Repeat the sound *yee joo*, *yee joo*, the numbers one and nine in Mandarin, for neck and/or back pain.

9. Repeat the sound *chee are*, *chee are*, the numbers seven and two in Mandarin, for problems related to the stomach.

For healing, always try to visualize white or golden light flowing into the top of the person's head, and concentrating that light in the area that most requires healing. Use your mind to see the person's body completely healthy. See the part that particularly requires healing to be one hundred percent perfect. Continue to visualize streams of white or gold light flooding the person's body and reaching out to their aura, perhaps one to two feet beyond the physical body.

Repeat the process as often as needed for relief. You should, of course, seek medical attention. Zhi Neng is a support, or complimentary, form of healing.

1	2	3	4	5	6	7	8	9
A	B	C	D	E	F	G	H	I
J	K	L	M	N	O	P	Q	R
S	T	U	V	W	X	Y	Z	

(Refer to Chapter 7)

1. **Vowels:** Inner Urge or Motivation (Soul Urge)
2. **Consonants:** Inner Self or Impression (Quiet Self)
3. **All Letters:** Outer Self (Expression, Destiny, Whole Self)

Name: _VIVIAN_ _Victoria_ _Zeh_

Vowels: _A i i_ _A i i o_ _e_   1. _4_

Consonants: _V V N_ _V c t r_ _Z h_   2. _4_

All Letters: _VIVIAN_ _Victoria_ _Zeh_   3. _5_

Descriptions:

1.

2.

3.

Significant Letters: _V_
Comments:

Name: _____ _____ _____

Vowels: _____ _____ _____   1. ____

Consonants: _____ _____ _____   2. ____

All Letters: _____ _____ _____   3. ____

Descriptions:

1.

2.

3.

Significant Letters:
Comments:

Name: _____ _____ _____

Vowels: _____ _____ _____   1. ____

Consonants: _____ _____ _____   2. ____

All Letters: _____ _____ _____   3. ____

Descriptions:

1.

2.

3.

Significant Letters:
Comments:

Use the various numerological values found in Worksheet No. 1 for each name or form of name and list below in the appropriate places.

Pg/Ltr Name

Vowels 1. ____
Consonants 2. ____
All letters 3. ____

CHALLENGES

1. (Motivation) First vowel—last vowel; subtract smaller value from greater value: ____ – ____ = ____

2. (Impression) First consonant—last consonant; subtract smaller value from greater: ____ – ____ = ____

3. (Expression) Add first challenge value to second challenge value: ____ + ____ = ____

Descriptions: (See list in Appendix 3)

1.

2.

3.

INCLUSION List values of all letters, with number of times they occur.

Use: 1 2 3 ____
4 5 6 ____   (Refer to list of meanings in Appendix 4)
7 8 9 ____

Descriptions:

HIDDEN PASSION From above, find greatest number of repetitions of values; perhaps second greatest, also. (See list of meanings in Appendix 5)
Descriptions:

HIDDEN PASSION CHALLENGES From the Inclusion chart, above, determine which number values are completely lacking (zero uses). Write them down:
____ ____ ____ ____ ____   (Look up the meaning[s] in Appendix 5.)
Description(s):

SUBCONSCIOUS SELF From above, determine number of zeros (missing values) and subtract from nine (9 – X) = SCS#.; 9 – ____ = ____ (See list in Appendix 5.)
Description:

CORNERSTONE First letter in first name ____ = ____ (Refer to list of basic meanings of numbers in Chapter 2.)
Description:

FIRST VOWEL Value of first vowel is the temperament or disposition: ____
(For meaning, see Appendix 5.)
Description:

KEY First name letters total value = Key #
Description:

Use the various numerological values found in worksheet No. 1 for each name or form of name and list below in the appropriate places.

Pg/Ltr   Name

KEY LETTER (Second Key) First letter in last name: ＿＿ = ＿＿
Description:

ECCENTRICITY Add day of birth number to Key number. ＿＿ + ＿＿ = ＿＿
Description:

BALANCE NUMBER Add values of three initials: ＿＿ + ＿＿ + ＿＿ = ＿＿
= ＿＿
Description: For meaning see Chapter 2.

CAPSTONE Last letter in first name ＿＿ is our manner of reaction to everyday life. For meaning, see Chapters 2 and 7.
Description:

KEYSTONE The middle letter of the first name (if odd number of letters). ＿＿
For meaning, see Appendix 5.
Description:

NAME CHARACTERISTIC Number of letters that make up the full name.
Description:

REALITY NUMBER
Description:

PLANES OF EXPRESSION
Description:

THE EXCURSION
Description:

Worksheet No. 4
Planes of Expression

GUIDE FOR PLACEMENT OF LETTERS
IN THE PLANES OF EXPRESSION

	EMOTIONAL	PHYSICAL	MENTAL	INTUITIVE	TOTALS
Creative	I O R Z	E	A	K	7
Grounded	—	D M	G L	C V	6
Vacilating	B S T X	W	H J N P	F Q U Y	13
Totals	8	4	7	7	26

NAME: _____ _____ _____

Place each letter of the full name, the number of times it actually occurs, in the proper space.

BLANK FORM FOR INSERTING
LETTERS OF THE NAME

	EMOTIONAL	PHYSICAL	MENTAL	INTUITIVE	TOTALS
Creative					
Grounded					
Vacilating					
Totals					

(Remember to divide the quantity of Es by two before totaling each line and column.)

DESCRIPTION OF THE FOUR PLANES

Emotional Plane:

People who are guided by their emotions rather than intellectual logic. They go by their feelings and sometimes appear to ignore the facts. These feeling, sentimental individuals possess creative imagination which aids their artistic expression.

Physical Plane:

These are the down-to-earth practical thinkers and doers. They would rather roll up their sleeves and get busy than plan it out. They are concerned with "reality" as they perceive it and have strong, positive opinions. They are the productive builders and workers.

Mental Plane:

These people evaluate, analyze, compare, weigh, consider with their intellect before proceeding. They want factual information ("Just the facts, ma'm!") on which to apply their reasoning power. These individuals are often technical writers, researchers, executives and business leaders.

Intuitive Plane:

These individuals are more psychic than most of us and are often guided by an inner source of knowledge or understanding. They are generally spiritual or even religious and just seem to "know" things that aren't apparent, or are inspired to follow a certain course of action.

THREE DIVISIONS OF THE
EXPRESSION PLANES

Creative:

These are the initiators, creative idea people and inspired leaders of others.

Grounded:

These stable, down-to-earth individuals are steady and "set" in their attitudes and situations. They have follow-through and will complete what they have started.

Vacillating:

These adaptable people can see more than one side of an issue, and are able to make quick changes and be involved in a number of things at a time.

APPENDIX 3
LIFE'S CHALLENGES

0. No specific challenge. Possibly all challenges, but of a lesser degree, within one lifetime. You have the choice of working on one or more, or all, challenges that are listed in the following items, one through eight. (There is no number nine challenge in a list of life's challenges.)

1. To become more of an individual, with independence and ambition, while not oppressing others. To keep the ego in check while developing self-confidence and inner drive. On the other hand, don't let another or others hold you back from all that you can be. Avoid laziness, selfishness, impatience and arrogance.

2. To learn to cooperate with others and overcome shyness while maintaining your own confidence and feeling of self-worth. Avoid being overemotional, but express your own

ideas and don't follow the leadership of others without good reason. Avoid superficial thought and action; pin down the details.

3. To learn to concentrate and not scatter your energies while developing your abilities for self-expression and social skills. Don't let fear of criticism stifle your creativity. Develop your speaking and writing skills, but use consideration and discretion lest you offend others and alienate those you wish to think well of you.

4. To accept and perform work with a positive attitude without becoming a workaholic who doesn't take time to enjoy life. On one hand, be productive, dependable, competent and punctual. One the other hand, don't allow yourself to get into a rut where work becomes your whole life.

5. To be adaptable and open to change without shirking your responsibilities or being irresponsible. Be discriminating and don't initiate change just for the sake of change or release from responsibility, but be open to realization of when things or people must be let go for your greater good. Be adaptable and accept variety, but make a strong effort to finish each thing you start.

6. To accept responsibilities, especially of marriage and home or of service to others, with good cheer, and to avoid being self-opinionated or self-righteous. Respect the opinions and desires of others. Live in beauty and harmony while trying to be of service to others.

7. To have faith and develop self-discipline and patience, to be alone without loneliness, and to avoid being aloof. To learn and then share your knowledge with others without a display of superiority. Cultivate relationships, but avoid too much partying or private overindulgence.

8. To develop the ability to use money and power wisely, neither in a wasteful nor miserly fashion. Avoid recklessness and inattention to detail. Strive for order and efficiency. Maintain worthy values and priorities, realizing that the riches of this planet are for everyone to share.

APPENDIX 4
INCLUSION

Some numerologists feel that the inclusion represents our experience from our past lives and what we are bringing with us into this present life. For those who do not accept the theory of reincarnation, the inclusion is viewed as a personality profile that indicates our abilities, talents, traits, strengths and weaknesses. Many numerologists think this is the most important analysis of the name.

For numbers that occur several times, the characteristic is especially strong. (Remember, E occurs so frequently in the English language that we should assign each E only one-half count. Otherwise almost everyone would have an overabundance of the five value.) A value (one through nine) that occurs one or two times indicates a normal degree of strength for that characteristic. Zero occurrences of a value indicate a lack of that characteristic in our makeup and where we should strive for development in this life.

Inclusion

ONE (Ego)—Self-reliance, ability to create, originality, determination, willpower, individuality and courage. An overabundance of ones can indicate a personality that wants to dominate others and is too full of pride and ego. The individual would probably be stubborn and opinionated. A shortage of ones may mean a lack of self-confidence, ambition, initiative or drive. However, this would be a person more easy to get along with, who is interested in others and what they have to say.

TWO (Subordinate)—Cooperative, associative, friendly and good mannered, works well with others in domestic and other areas. An overabundance of twos could mean a person who is too dependent upon others, who may see the individual as a bit of a drain or burden. Such a person, however, would be a good friend and a peacemaker, albeit overly sensitive and emotional. A lack of twos shows a lack of sensitivity and consideration for others, and the possible inability to work in a cooperative effort. Such a person might be inflexible, edgy or downright crabby.

THREE (Expressive)—Self-expressive, artistically creative, outgoing, joyful, social, friendly, enthusiastic, with the ability to write or express verbally. An overabundance of threes might indicate a party person with a boastful nature, but without real purpose. The individual could be extravagant, impatient, overly talkative and, to an excessive degree, seeking the approval and admiration of others. A lack of threes could mean a withdrawn person, possibly with an inferiority complex, who shuns social situations and lacks the ability to express.

FOUR (Work)—A hard worker, who is attentive to details. Ability to concentrate and follow through with purpose in an organized way. An overabundance of fours indicates a workaholic who is immersed in endless tasks and details. He or she would have a narrow outlook and be resistant to participating in enjoyable activities of life, thinking them too frivolous. A lack of fours suggests a person who dislikes any sort of mundane or detail work and is impatient with routine.

FIVE (Freedom)—Adaptable, freedom loving, acceptable to change, enjoys variety and even adventure. An overabundance of fives denotes a person who may be restless and irresponsible, especially in domestic situations and, thinking the grass is greener elsewhere, initiating change without good reason. It could indicate excessive sexual involvement. It suggests a person who may not carry an action through to completion due to the tendency to shift interest frequently. A lack of fives implies a person who is a bit of a stick-in-the-mud, resistant to change, unable to adapt and who may restrict others. This person may tend to be jealous, lacking in experience and understanding, and could be a loner, lacking any joy of life. (Note: Since the letter E occurs so often in the English language, allow only one-half occurrence of five for each E.)

SIX (Responsibility)—Accepting of his or her situation in life, a responsible person, especially regarding home and family, who loves beautiful surroundings. A service-oriented humanitarian, could be involved in the welfare of others, and desires harmony, balance and fairness. An overabundance of sixes suggests being too restricted in interests other than home and family, leading to an inflexible, dogmatic nature, unable to entertain new concepts or ideas. It suggests a very traditional, possibly fanatical, nature. A lack of sixes denotes an unrealistic outlook with a dislike of responsibility. It implies that the individual is self-centered and may be domineering.

SEVEN (Knowledge)—Understanding, investigative, analytical, usually a keen mind with zeal to explore the unknown.

While a seeker after facts and the truth, the individual is usually compassionate and accepts God. An overabundance of sevens, which is rare, portends an individual with vast intellect such as a great scientist or inventor. He or she would likely be taciturn and not friendly with many, except a few intellectuals with similar interests. A lack of sevens, which is quite usual, signals a person with little interest in spiritual matters or any degree of inner faith. This individual would be rather outgoing and may be somewhat impatient and impulsive.

EIGHT (Material)—a healthy respect for money and items of value. They are usually executive types who manage well, especially in business and financial areas. They are generally efficient, organized, and enterprising, with good reasoning ability. An overabundance of eights signals an individual who may be materialistic and money- or power-hungry. He or she may be so submerged in business or finance for the accumulation of wealth that other areas of life go begging. A lack of eights signals an individual with too little concern with the material aspects of life. He or she may work at a job, profession or business with too little concern about financial return, and may do poorly with money management. Such an individual could wind up financially dependent on others if this is not guarded against.

NINE (Compassion)—A person who cares about his or her fellow man with tolerance and kindness. A humanitarian who is understanding, sympathetic and giving. An overabundance of nines could indicate a person so concerned with the problems of mankind that he or she cannot live a normal, happy life. It signals a person who is overly sensitive and emotional, giving too much to others (often to their detriment) to the point of shortchanging themselves. On the other hand, this individual can be very unaccepting of the opinions or advice of others, and always determined to do things their own way. A lack of nines marks a person who seems a bit callous about the suffering of others and who should develop discernment of when some compassion is called for. Often this lesson is learned during the current lifetime, when this person is in a situation where he or she needs some help from others.

APPENDIX 5
HIDDEN PASSION

Also know as the Ruling Passion or Secret Desire, this is a powerful inner impulse that motivates strong desire, expression and action along particular lines. Find the Hidden Passion by selecting from the Inclusion chart the number or numbers that occur most. In some cases there may be two or even three numbers that occur more frequently (at least three times) than others. Remember to divide the number of occurrences of five due to the letter E by two. If a number occurs four or more times, it is considered a strong influence. Refer to the following list of Hidden Passion numbers:

ONE: Passion or drive for self.
TWO: Passion or drive for companionship, belonging, association or affiliation.

THREE: Passion or drive for creativity, self-expression, and originality.

FOUR: Passion or drive for work, productivity, or accomplishment.

FIVE: Passion or drive for freedom, independence, change and variety.

SIX: Passion or drive for responsibility, position, marriage, home and family.

SEVEN: Passion or drive for knowledge, truth, spiritual laws, understanding and wisdom.

EIGHT: Passion or drive for material gain, money and power.

NINE: Passion or drive for spiritual love, universal knowledge and self-reliance.

CHALLENGES TO THE HIDDEN PASSION

A lack of any of the above numerological values indicates areas where we must develop to make up for deficiencies in certain character aspects in which we were weak coming into this lifetime. Refer to the following list for where you should apply effort to offset the lack of certain numbers, that is, zero occurrences, in your name. One occurrence indicates a slight weakness.

HIDDEN PASSION CHALLENGES

ONE: A need to develop self-confidence, be decisive, stand on your own two feet, be ambitious and outspoken; put forth your ideas.

TWO: A need to associate, work and cooperate with others. Release introvert tendencies; learn to converse and socialize.

THREE: A need to develop self-expression, creativity, speaking and writing skills.

FOUR: A need for a positive attitude toward work, and the development of organization, planning, scheduling, efficiency and attention to details.

FIVE: A need to accept change and become adaptable, to enjoy freedom and variety without shirking responsibilities or causing distress to others.

SIX: A need to accept responsibility, especially with home and family, to develop patience and to be of service to others.

SEVEN: A need to develop curiosity and desire to learn, acquire knowledge, patiently gain understanding and wisdom, and eventually (in this lifetime or another) experience spiritual and cosmic truths.

EIGHT: A need to learn how to handle money, develop business savvy, develop a respect for and understanding of material value. To take control of your financial affairs and develop the ability to delegate and lead others in a businesslike manner.

NINE: To become a sympathetic, compassionate person who has tolerance for and understanding of the failings of others. To be mindful that not everyone is as fortunate as we are and that many people need a helping hand. To remember that, "As ye do it unto the least of these, ye do it unto me."

SUBCONSCIOUS SELF

Note: 1, 2, and 3 never occur in this analysis, according to numerological authorities. However, as can be seen in Chapter 7, it was not difficult to find a fairly common first and last name that contained only three numerological values. Even though we don't ascribe to the value of this particular name analysis, it's included for your consideration.

4. Five karmic lessons are involved. It's felt that this individual would be completely awash in concern with details, incapable of effective action and unable to make clear-cut decisions.
5. This individual would be high-strung, and incapable of any real responsibility. There would be much spinning of wheels without getting anywhere.
6. There would be much concern with family and home. Only when this area of life was settled and sound, could attention be given to other matters.
7. This individual would be hard to reach on a personal level. He or she might appear to be a snob and detached from others. This person would mull things over inwardly and could tend toward alcoholism.
8. This person would tend to be materially oriented, detached and matter-of-fact, but would be reliable and solid in almost any situation.
9. With no Karmic lessons to resolve, this individual would be his or her own person, with little concern for things or people in life. He or she would just not attach much importance to the everyday circumstances of life.

FIRST VOWEL

Note: Y is often used as a vowel in the English language. Refer to the beginning of the section on Analysis of the Name in Chapter 7. In the case of diphthongs (two vowels together) the first is dominant, but modified by the characteristics of the second vowel. There is also a distinction involving a long vowel compared to the short form. The short form is considered to be less forceful or strong in nature, but will act more quickly and over a shorter period of time, and is generally more adaptable and flexible.

A (1)—Intellectual and original, with the drive of the one. Can be selfish and domineering in nature. Leadership, innovation, ambition and creativity are among its characteristics.

E (5)—Physically active, freedom-loving and adaptable, these people desire and enjoy change and variety. They wish to enjoy life in all its aspects and, generally, are very lively and interesting. On the downside, they are not the best marriage material since they're not prone to desire the settled life of home and family.

I (9)—Emotional, understanding and caring, this group of individuals are the humanitarians who try to make the world better for others as well as for themselves. They are usually reliable, stable and unselfish.

O (6)—Secretive, self-contained and sympathetic, these responsible individuals are ideal in a life of home and family. They love beauty and are cooperative in work and relationships. They must guard against domination of their families.

U (3)—Intuitive, creative, talented and artistic, these friendly and sociable people are the most pleasant to be around. They are quick, cooperative workers and generally excel at written or verbal communication.

Y (7)—Seekers of knowledge, these quiet individuals are the thinkers, researchers, inventors and teachers. They tend to have only a few close friends and their search for truth often takes them into matters of the spirit, God and religions.

Eccentricity

1. Would be self-reliant, using own strength and capabilities to overcome or accomplish. Prefers to go it alone.

2. Would seek help from others, to overcome or achieve in a cooperative action, feeling two heads are better than one.

3. Would come up with a creative idea or concept to overcome or accomplish.

4. Would strive, with diligent effort, to work his or her way out of the situation.

5. Would seek to change the situation or escape from it. Would take a chance with some new or innovative action.

6. Would accept the responsibility and obligation, as long as home and family were secure and safe; would fall back upon them for support and comfort.

7. Would go within to analyze and evaluate the situation. Would refer to the inner self with prayer and meditation, anticipating inspiration and spiritual guidance.

8. Would consider the material aspects, primarily, and try to resolve the situation along the lines of value and money. Would use planning and organization to help resolve the situation.

9. Would consider the overall ramifications of the situation and consider the consequences to all concerned. Decision would be based on humanitarian considerations.

KEYSTONE

This is the middle letter of the first name (only for those with an odd number of letters.)

A Denotes mental ability.

B Portends cooperative, constructive outlook.

C Implies creativity.

D May lack follow-through on work at hand, but will strive for approval.

E Signifies analytical mind, excellent for research.

F Very firm and closed in beliefs and opinions.

G Often shouldering great burdens with solitary determination.

H Marks a sharp business person.

I Aware of guidance from his or her higher mind, can inspire others.

J Fair; seeks a system of justice and balance with financial return.

K A good teacher who extends a helping hand to others.

L Unusually well balanced with good reasoning ability and a seeker of justice.

M Signifies an active life style; good worker.

N An adaptable, versatile humanitarian.

O Introspective and strong-willed.

P Power-loving loner with intuitive abilities.

Q Indicates a responsible executive-type who lifts the spirits of others.

R Represents one who, unselfishly, stimulates thought and action of others.

S Signifies a self-sufficient individual with a shrewd and cunning mind.

T Denotes a gentle person with originality and a quick, sharp mind.

U Indicates a conservative, detail-oriented nature, complete unto itself.

V A discreet and cautious builder with insight.

W Adaptable and versatile, but often too scattered.

X Brave, but considerate and talented.

Y Sympathetic, perceptive and gentle, with an humble nature.

Z One who has spiritual insight and can bring understanding to others.

APPENDIX 6
NAME CHARACTERISTIC

There are two methods of finding the name characteristic. First, the short way, by reducing the total number of letters in the full name to a single digit (except in the case of eleven or twenty-two) and finding the interpretation in the first, short list. The second method is to use the full number of letters without reducing and look up the characteristic in the second, long, list.

Reduced List
1. An original thinker with the power of concentration to a point of being inflexible and short-tempered with others.
2. Well-organized and detail-oriented; may be too cut off from others.
3. Self-expressive and creative; seeks approval.
4. Conservative, conscientious, productive worker; may try to ignore problems.

5. Lover of variety and change; may lack continuity of purpose.

6. Loves to provide and inhabit beautiful surroundings; may be oppressive to others.

7. Often a professional person who specializes in a particular area, such as a medical doctor; may be too aloof and overly sensitive to criticism of status or social standing.

8. Must refrain from bias or influence in judgment; capable of mediation of disputes.

9. An authoritative individual who might be edgy due to inner conflict, but generally understanding and pleasant.

11. Usually a shy, spiritual person who can teach and inspire others.

22. Great breadth of intellect and understanding, a person who never tires of his or her work.

Name Characteristic—Long List

10. Self-confident, with originality and carry-through, but not very popular.

11. Sympathetic and understanding, with creative artistic abilities; may be taken advantage of by others.

12. Self-expressive and artistically creative, looking for encouragement by others, but may meet with derision and even be made a scapegoat due to envy by some.

13. Conservative hard worker who may encounter sudden change and upheaval in life.

14. A life of change, variety and movement, with much sexuality; must guard against harm from others.

15. A balanced harmonious life with elements of beauty and benefit from others.

16. Be on guard for personal weakness and hard times. Personal relationships may be disappointing.

17. Spiritual nature, usually achieves financial success and public acclaim.

18. May be inner conflict between spiritual nature and material considerations.

19. Portends success, happiness and honor.

20. Denotes lack of success for material gain.

21. Reaches success late in life.

22. May lack discrimination in evaluation of others, leading to erroneous judgment.

23. A very fortunate number denoting success with help of influential people.

24. Indicates gain from members of the opposite sex; be careful of large animals.

25. Signifies rough going early in life, but ultimate success, with water being an especially fortunate element.

26. Signals financial success in public affairs.

27. Pleasant personality who achieves power and authority.

29. Signals warning of an uncertain life and not to be quick to trust others. Problems with opposite sex are likely.

30. Can be a pleasant life if other numerological aspects are not unfavorable.

31. Take the necessary steps to avoid financial lack and loneliness.

32. Implies a life with close friends, but guard against immoral behavior. There may be a connection with magic.

33. A conservative life, but avoid being involved in acts against the government.

34. Portends a mystical life shrouded in secrecy.

35. Implies a life of financial ease through inheritance.

36. Denotes a life that presents struggle with poor times and good times, but ultimately success and authority are achieved.

37. Signifies a life with good personal relationships.

38. Be warned to avoid separation and divorce.

39. A very fortunate life with favorable personal relationships, good health and long life.

40. Presents a life with strong literary aspects and conservative finances.

41. Indicates detachment from mundane matters.

42. Of a humanitarian, religious nature; helpful to others, but guard against possibly fatal accidents or other dangerous situations while still in the prime of life.

43. Warns of an unfortunate life involving military service and war or civil uprising.

44. Success in the material as well as other areas, but could involve loss in personal life.

Reality Number

1. Ambitious, original, creative and opinionated, these individuals are leaders, executives and directors who are often involved in large enterprises. They have strong convictions and are very active in their work, through which they reach success by following their own ideas. They must realize that their ego and pride can lead to poor relations with associates and others in their lives.

2. Cooperative, pleasant and patient, these people are often consultants or arbitrators, and frequently involved in finance or medicine. They are generally interested in the fine arts and often intuitive or psychic. They reach success through their ability to work hard and steadily rather than through connections since they tend to be overly shy or separated. Others may try to take advantage of them.

3. Creative, artistic and communicative, these individuals are often writers, artists or entertainers and sometimes involved with investment media such as real estate or the stock market. Self-expression is the key word for these imaginative people, who are frequently public speakers, singers or composers. Public life is another likely area for them. They must guard against scattering their talents to the detriment of their success and being overly self-important, impatient or extravagant.

4. Practical, persistent, hardworking and honest, these men and women can be found in business, science, art or religion. They expect to work for success, with patience and attention to detail as they use their reasoning power and ideas. They must guard against being workaholics who shun social activities and spend too little time with their families. These energetic people should also avoid becoming domineering, narrow-minded or resentful.

5. Versatile, adaptable and independent, these individuals are reporters, entertainers, lawyers, and in advertising, travel and promotional businesses. They excel where foresight and getting there first are important. They must guard against scattering their energies, becoming restless, critical or self-important. They are attractive to the opposite sex and enjoy an active life of variety and change.

6. Considerate, responsible and service-oriented, these lovers of home and family are often doctors, engineers, lawyers, painters, decorators, landscapers, teachers and actors. They also succeed in service occupations involving social services, hospitals and charitable organizations. They should guard against being domineering, stubborn or interfering.

7. Seekers of wisdom, introspective, private and innovative, these studious individuals are frequently scientists, research-

ers, inventors and mystics. They also succeed as historians, detectives, surgeons, technicians, chemists, statisticians and in involvement with the spiritual. Marriage can be a problem due to their desire for solitary study or research. They should guard against being too cut off from others and becoming nervous, critical, rebellious, confused or even alcoholic.

8. Achievers, managers, philosophers and advisers, these reliable individuals are often analysts, directors, psychologists, supervisors, architects, resort owners and explorers. They also succeed as publishers, civil engineers and real-estate agents. They must not lose the balance of a life of worthwhile purpose versus material acquisition or they could lose what they've gained. They also have to guard against becoming thoughtless, miserly, unreliable or power hungry.

9. Understanding, generous and sympathetic, these humanitarians make good teachers, ministers, philanthropists, writers, speakers, artisans and craftsmen. To succeed, this number requires a strong-willed effort to replace material involvements with the spiritual, to seek higher planes of awareness and to help those in need through their sympathy and generosity. The rewards will be there. These people should guard against being impractical, selfish or overemotional.

11. If these individuals can live up to the demands of this master number, which is a higher octave of the two, they will be tuned into spiritual truths and cosmic knowledge which they are to share with others. These people are often ministers, mediums or psychics, often in the roles of religious or spiritual leaders. They must guard against reluctance to share knowledge, loss of faith or being dishonest or immoral in any way.

22. This master number, a higher octave of four, indicates master

builders who work to provide for humanity on a broad scale. These people are often architects who create large projects for people in general, or brilliant scientists, researchers or doctors who provide benefit to humanity. They must guard against failure to heed their inner, spiritual guidance.

INDEX

El Greco, 141
elements, 22–33, 23, 24, 29, 30
Elements (Euclid), 13
eleven (number), 9, 20, 31–32
  alphabet values and, 129
  as birth date, 39–40
  Chinese numerology and, 175
  Inner Self and, 136
  Inner Urge or Motivation and, 134
  life cycle (sub-path) and, 126
  life path and, 113
  name characteristic of, 200
  Outer Self or Expression and, 137
  personal days and, 107
  personal month and, 106
  personal year and, 97, 98, 104
  as reality number, 204
  weight loss and, 92
Eliyahu of Vilna, 88
Emerson, Ralph Waldo, 141, 142
emotional plane, 181
England, 12
enjoyment, 99–100, 110
Enochian mathematics, 16
epidemics, 96
equality, 36
equinoxes, 13
esoteric teachings, 18
Euclid, 13, 18, 141
Euler, Leonhard, 141
Euripedes, 141
expression planes, 180–82
extravagance, 118
eye contact, 172

family, 100, 194, 195
  alphabet values and, 141
  eccentricity and, 196
  as hidden passion, 192
  life cycles and, 107, 109, 112, 115, 116, 124
  lucky numbers and, 42, 44
famine, 96
fanaticism, 31–32, 137, 188
Farrell, Charles, 141
fathers, 117
Feiffer, Jules, 90

feminine numbers, 22, 23
Feng Shui, 174
Ferrer, José, 88
fidelity, 84
Fields, W. C., 90
finance, 95, 102–3, 135, 164, 165, 193, 202
  See also money
first initial, 2
first vowel, in names, 2, 152, 195–96
Five Elements, 174
five (number), 20, 26–27
  Chinese numerology and, 175
  hidden passion and, 192, 193
  inclusion and, 188
  Inner Self and, 135
  Inner Urge or Motivation and, 133
  life cycle (sub-path) and, 120–21
  life path and, 110–11
  name characteristic of, 200
  Outer Self or Expression and, 137
  personal days and, 107
  personal month and, 105
  as personal year, 100–101
  as reality number, 203
  success and, 162–63
flexibility, 44
Florida water, 53
Fonda, Henry, 141
food, 86, 90–93, 161
foresight, 144
formative period, 114–27
fortunate cycles, 60
Foster, Preston, 141
four (number), 11, 20, 25–26
  hidden passion and, 192, 193
  inclusion and, 187–88
  Inner Self and, 135
  Inner Urge or Motivation and, 133
  life cycle (sub-path) and, 119–20
  life path and, 110
  name characteristic of, 199
  Outer Self or Expression and, 136–37
  personal days and, 107
  personal month and, 105
  as personal year, 100
  as reality number, 203
  success and, 162

inspiration, 35, 78, 104, 106, 113, 126
integers, 14
integrity, 84
Intelligence Quotient (IQ), 79
intolerance, 23, 29, 110, 112
introspection, 85, 104, 115
introversion, 45
introvesion, 122
intuition, 6–7, 28, 31, 103, 110, 113
    first vowel and, 195
    gambling hunches, 52–53
    lucky numbers and, 38, 44
    reality numbers and, 202
intuitive plane, 182
irrational numbers, 15
Islamic mathematicians, 16

jealousy, 23, 36, 44, 83, 110, 137, 188
Jefferson, Thomas, 143
Jesus, 11, 16, 19
Jewish mysticism, 16, 87–88
Jillian, Ann, 90
Job (biblical), 61
Jones, Dean, 90
judgment, 112, 124, 200
Jung, Carl Gustav, 143
Jupiter (planet), 24
justice, 36, 46, 197
Justinian, Emperor, 16

Kabbalah/Kabbalism, 16, 87–88, 139
Kahn, Madeline, 143
karma, 70, 194
Kaye, Danny, 89
Keaton, Diane, 88
Kelly, Edward, 16
Kennedy, John F., 143
key, 152
key letter, in names, 152
keystone, 153, 197–98
keywords, 21, 83, 135–36
Khayyam, Omar, 144
Khufu (pharaoh), 17
Kissinger, Henry, 143
Kitt, Eartha, 89
knowledge, 28, 111, 122, 123, 126

as challenge, 193
first vowel and, 196
as hidden passion, 192
inclusion and, 188–89
inner source of, 182
kunzite, 58

LaRosa, Julius, 88
Last Supper, 11
Laurie, Piper, 90
law of flow, 54, 158
laziness, 112, 183
leadership, 21, 29, 32, 77, 135
    first vowel and, 195
    full number value and, 140, 142
    Inner Urge and, 132
    lucky numbers and, 36, 39, 43, 45
left brain, 40
Leigh, Janet, 4
Leno, Jay, 143
Leo (astrological sign), 59
León, Moses de, 87
Letterman, David, 143
Libra (astrological sign), 59
libraries, 96
license plate numbers, 34–35, 53
life cycles, 108–27
Life Path Number, 154
Lincoln, Abraham, 140
Lo Shu grid, 173–74
London, Jack, 89
loneliness, 184, 201
Lopez, Nancy, 88
Loren, Sophia, 54
Lotto, 35, 55, 61
Lotto: How to Wheel a Fortune
    (Howard), 61
love, 37, 40, 80
loyalty, 84
lucky numbers, 9, 34–47
Luria, Isaac, 87

MacLaine, Shirley, 143
McQueen, Butterfly, 88
magic, 14, 201
magic squares, 173–74

polarities, 22–33
Pollock, Jackson, 90
positive energy, 60–61
possessiveness, 75
power, 29, 124, 185, 197
    lover's or mate's birth date and, 81,
        85
    lucky numbers and, 38
    name analysis and, 134, 144
prayers, 50, 52
Presley, Elvis, 88
pride, 167, 187
primary numbers, 20–31
priming the pump, 51
Principal, Victoria, 88
priorities, 85
productive period, 114–27
productivity, 25, 135, 192
promiscuity, 28
proportion, 13, 19
psychic ability, 6, 7, 39, 103, 126, 202,
    204
psychology, 46
Ptolemy, 16
public service, 104
pyramids, 12, 17
Pythagoras, 2–3, 14–15, 18, 19
Pythagorean Theorem, 13, 15

Qi Gong, 92, 174
quartz, 59
Quetzalcoatl (Aztec god), 144
Quinn, Anthony, 144

racetrack, 55
Raitt, John, 89
Rand, Sally, 88
Reagan, Ronald, 145
reality number, 156, 202–5
reciprocity, 19
recklessness, 75, 185
red apple fragrance, 59
Redgrave, Vanessa, 90
refurbishing homes, 101, 105
relationships, 101, 103, 184, 200
religion, 10, 14, 161, 196, 203

life cycles and, 123, 124
    universal year and, 95, 96
responsibility, 27, 41, 43, 46, 111, 135
    acceptance of, 184
    as challenge, 193
    eccentricity and, 196
    full number value and, 146
    as hidden passion, 192
    inclusion and, 188
restlessness, 74
restriction, 26, 29
retirement, 121, 123, 124, 125
Retton, Mary Lou, 90
revelation, 113
Revere, Paul, 88
Rickover, Hyman, 90
right brain, 40, 58
Rivera, Chita, 90
Roach, Hal, 89
Roberts, Oral, 90
Robinson, Jackie, 90
Rogers, Ginger, 3
Rooney, Andy, 89
Roosevelt, Franklin D., 90
Roosevelt, Theodore, 145
Rosicrucians, 60, 88
Ross, Betsy, 88
ruling passion. See hidden passion
Rush, Barbara, 88

Sade (singer), 89
Sagittarius (astrological sign), 59
Sales, Soupy, 88, 172
Sandburg, Carl, 88
Saturn (planet), 30, 102
Scavullo, Francesco, 89
School of Athens, 18
Schumann Resonance, 2
Schwarzenegger, Arnold, 5
Schweitzer, Albert, 89
science, 28, 38, 126, 174, 203
science fiction, 46
Scorpio (astrological sign), 59
seasons, prediction of, 13
secret desire. See hidden passion
seers, 2
Sefer Yezira, 16, 87

ABOUT THE AUTHORS

JOYCE KELLER is an internationally known psychic, healer, counselor, lecturer and hypnotherapist, who is also the author of *Calling All Angels*, and the "Angel Series" of American Media's Micro Mags. She has hosted her own television show for over fifteen years. On the air since 1986, she continues to host America's longest-running intuitive advice and interview radio show, on WGBB, 1240 AM, Long Island, New York. She can be found on three web sites, www.joycekeller.com, www.WGBB.com, and www.lifetimetv.com, under "My Horoscope." Ms. Keller appears frequently on major TV shows, such as *Oprah*, *Regis*, *Sally Jessy Raphael*, *Entertainment Tonight*, and many other TV and radio shows. She was recently featured in *The 100 Top Psychics in America*, and is listed in all editions of *Who's Who*. Ms. Keller resides in West Islip, New York and New York City.

JACK KELLER is a licensed New York State Professional Engineer who works as a consultant and expert witness for attorneys on personal-injury accident cases. He cohosts with Joyce on her radio show. He has lectured, demonstrated and taught yoga, past-life regression, astrology, numerology and other metaphysical subjects for many years. He appears in most recent editions of *Who's Who*, and resides in West Islip, New York and New York City.